Succeeding in
InformationTechnology

Succeeding in
Information Technology

Tips and Strategies To Be An IT Superstar

MICHAEL LEONARDICH

ISBN: 979-8-89109-469-7 - paperback

ISBN: 979-8-89109-471-0 - ebook

Library of Congress Control Number: 2023921124

First Edition December 2023

Introduction

This book started as a story of my forty-five-year career in Information Technology focusing on my major projects and accomplishments. I quickly realized it would be more valuable if I explained the strategies that contributed to my success so that others can use them to advance their own careers.

This is not another boring step-by-step how-to book for beginners interested in a career in Information Technology. Instead, it is a collection of real-life experiences and the underlying strategies that, when followed, contribute to a rewarding and successful life journey.

Those of you with project management experience will know the desired outcome of any endeavor is to get it done on time, on budget, and with high quality. The reality is that most managers are faced with unrealistic timeframes, insufficient funding, incomplete requirements, and lack of resources. Well, I have been given seemingly impossible tasks by CEOs and have been told, "Money is no object—you have an open checkbook. Just get it done!" At first, this sounds like a manager's "dream come true," but when the realization of what you have been asked to do sinks in, it scares the heck out of you.

This book includes some of these projects and the strategies it took to be successful.

Dedication

This book would not have been possible if it weren't for my wife, Suzanne, and our two boys, Daniel and Joseph. These projects frequently kept me away from them for countless nights, weekends, holidays, and even weeks. At the beginning of our courtship, I am sure Suzanne had no idea what it was like entering into a relationship with someone who was on call twenty-four hours a day supporting technical infrastructures that kept companies running. I will be forever grateful to them for their understanding and loving support.

I would also like to dedicate this to my parents who kept me pointed in the right direction and taught me the values of hard work, dedication, and taking pride in my accomplishments. I am truly sorry for putting gun powder in your ash trays one memorable April Fool's Day – yes, it was me!

Table of Contents

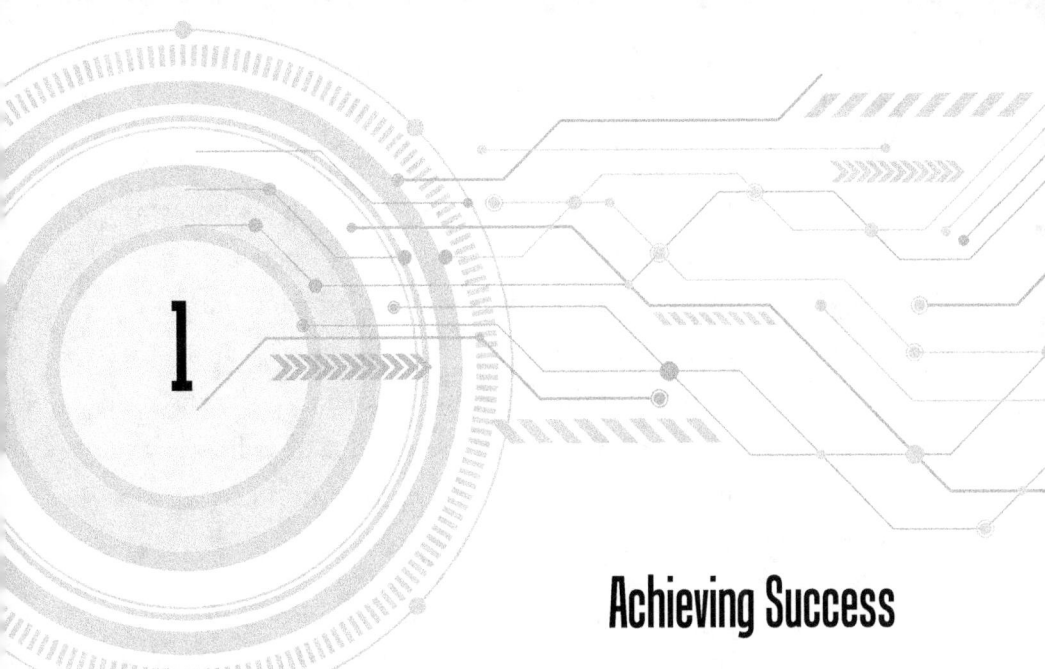

Achieving Success

Everyone wants to be successful. Some measure success by how much money they make, the size of their house, the type of car they drive, becoming famous, owning their own company, finding a soul mate, or just being happy about what they have accomplished. There have been thousands of self-help books about the topic. However, this book may be the only one that focuses on being successful in the Information Technology profession.

It can be argued that IT is one of the most complex and unique professions that exists in the business world. Just like all the other professions, it is not for everyone. Just because someone has a penchant for technology, doesn't mean they will be good at it. It requires a combination of both hard and soft skills, and above all else, an analytical mind. Success in IT does not mean mastering all the technologies, after all, there are too many. Some people like coding or web development, others prefer networking or infrastructure.

The great part about IT is that it has so many different facets or specialties. Just look at the technology section in a bookstore and you will see books on coding, system design, programming languages, hardware engineering, networking, and many more. No one starts out with the intent of being an IT professional—they start out pursuing something that interests them. As they become exposed to more facets of the profession, and their skills improve, they may change specialties. This book helps them focus on what is important to remember as time progresses.

Working in IT can be addictive because of the lure of the next new and great piece of hardware or software. There is a danger where one focuses solely on a specific piece of technology and ignores all the rest. In one company I worked for, there was someone who was an expert on an IBM piece of technology, the 3705 communications controller. He had several years of experience with the device and knew everything there was to know about it. Even IBM called him to resolve complex problems. When IBM announced the device was being replaced with new technology, he became extremely despondent and felt there was nothing else to live for and took his own life. Don't let this happen to you. There's nothing wrong with becoming a generalist—you will find you will always be in demand and well on your way to achieving success.

Kindle The Passion

Everyone knows someone who they consider a professional. It could be a doctor, a lawyer, a contractor, or anyone else that has mastered their craft and is dedicated to doing the best job possible. Whatever the profession, they have a sincere passion for it.

Just like every other college freshman, the choice of a major is difficult. There are very few 18-year-olds that know what they want to be when they grow up, and that included me. So, when the time came to make a choice, I reflected on high school and chose chemistry, which I enjoyed and excelled at. (I received the Bank of America Award for Science at graduation.) It didn't take long for me to realize I may not have made the right choice. This major required me to take not only chemistry courses, but also physics, calculus, and algebra. Besides attending classes, there were multiple three-hour labs per week. It was overwhelming, and even chemistry, which I enjoyed in high school, became drudgery.

Toward the end of my first semester at the University of San Francisco, a new friend of mine, Ernie from El Paso, Texas, stopped by my dorm room to chat. After a while, Ernie mentioned he needed to go to the computer center to work on his programming homework. He showed me a deck of computer cards full of small rectangular holes and some writing on the top of each card that he explained was a programming language called Fortran IV. This immediately caught my interest since I had never seen a computer before, so I went with him. The closest I had ever gotten to a computer was the punch card that came with the family's phone bill every month.

Ernie showed me USF's IBM 1130 computer which was not much larger than a big oak desk. I watched Ernie put his card deck in the card reader and enter a command on the console that resembled an IBM Selectric™ typewriter. One by one, the cards were pulled into the reader and were deposited in a hopper. Moments later the printer began to chatter and produced multiple pages of 11" by 17" green bar paper. Wow! I had Ernie explain his program to me, after which I realized I wanted to be part of this. The next day, I went to the campus bookstore and bought a Fortran IV Programming book. It was not long before I was writing simple programs. I spent so much time in the computer center, I soon became known by the teaching assistants (TA's). Before the semester ended, I changed my major to math since the college's computer classes were in the math department.

I took the intro to computers and programming class during my second freshman semester. I was in love! I couldn't get enough of programming. I soon found myself answering questions from my fellow classmates, which was noticed by the head TA. I was offered a job as a TA the next semester and as a sophomore became the youngest TA in the department.

My first experience as a TA was quite memorable. There I was standing in front of a room full of students with the IBM 1130 off to the side. Suddenly, the door flew open and in came five or six of my fellow TAs. Without uttering a word, they opened the covers of the 1130 and began flipping multiple switches, which disabled it. They left as quickly and silently as they entered, but this time with an evil grin on their faces. It took a while to undo the damage, but I got the computer working again. This was their way of welcoming me to the team. So much for my first teaching experience.

The supervisor over the computer center and the TAs was a university employee named Michael. One of Michael's duties was to write programs for registration, payroll, and other processes. He wrote a routine that would automatically execute whenever a student ran a program. It would print a banner on the first pages of the student's output. It became very annoying as the banner would read "Hurray, finals are here" or some other message just to annoy the students. After a few weeks of seeing these banners on every printout, I decided to figure out how this worked. I discovered Michael's program and traced its logic. Michael used a password to activate the program. After pouring through the program, I found the password and changed it. From that day on the banner read, "We've done it, we've ravished the maiden." Michael repeatedly tried his password to change the banner, but of course, he was not successful. A few days later, the program was removed. What fun. I may have been the first "hacker" in the university's history.

When Junior year began, the university replaced the 1130 with an RCA Spectra 70/46 time sharing computer. The computer was massive—it took up the space formerly used by three classrooms. I was offered a part-time job as a student computer operator, which I quickly accepted. Little did I know at the time, this job provided unrestricted access to the computer, which would come in very handy.

By this time, I already had a reputation for being a good programmer. It was a remarkably interesting time at USF since computers were still in their infancy and very few students and teachers had programming skills. I remember taking an accounting class where the professor told us we were going to have to produce a set of working papers for a small business as our final exam. After a few classes, I realized it would be a simple matter to write a program that could produce these working papers. I approached the professor and offered to automate the process. He was thrilled. Like many other teachers, he wanted to join the computer age, but didn't know how. After a bit of negotiation, he agreed to excuse me from classes and homework and the final. If I were successful, I would get an A. If not, I would fail the course. Needless to say, I got that A.

A similar opportunity presented itself in linguistics class. During the first class, the professor mentioned he had obtained a reel of computer tape containing the entire dictionary. He wanted to do some research on words and letters in the dictionary but didn't know how to access the information on the tape. Well, that was all it took—shortly thereafter, I was writing a series of programs for the professor and was excused from going to class and taking tests. Oh, yes, lest we forget, another A.

One of the upper division classes we had to take was systems programming. This focused on computer operating systems, software internals, file system architecture, etc. One of our lab assignments was to create an ISAM (Index Sequential Access Method) file manually. We had to use operating system commands to find and allocate disk space and then create the file's header and indexes by entering one byte at a time. These bytes were in hexadecimal, which was a bit tricky. When we finished creating the file, we were to print it to test it.

One evening, I completed my file and issued the command to print it. I walked across the hall to the computer center to retrieve my printout, and as luck would have it, the mainframe had crashed, impacting dozens of students. It took the computer operator about an hour to restart the machine. I then printed my file again, and to my surprise, the mainframe crashed again! This was getting annoying. I noticed the campus systems programmer was now in the computer center hovering over the console, going over multiple pages of core dump. My fellow students and I were getting frustrated and wondered when the computer would be back up. Well, you guessed it—the computer came back up, I printed my file, and boom! Down it went.

Hmmm. My mom didn't raise any dumb children. It did not take long to figure out my file must have been causing the mainframe to crash. Back to the terminal I went and poured over my file in excruciating detail. There it was, the index I had created was flawed. When the mainframe tried to print it, the code misdirected the operating system to a bogus memory address which it did not know how to handle. A system crash was the result. I rebuilt the index and nervously printed it again. This time it worked. They never found out my file was the cause. It was quite a learning experience, to say the least.

It was around this time USF created the Computer Science department, and all of us mislabeled math majors became Computer Science majors, the first in USF history! In 1972, there were less than 10 CS graduates. A rare commodity indeed.

One of the classes I took was an advanced programming course. Our professor said there would be no homework or tests. Our grade would be dependent on a single computer program we would write based on specifications provided by the professor. If it ran successfully and produced the desired result, the student would get an 'A'. If it failed, the grade would be an 'F'.

Throughout the year, the professor taught us advanced programming techniques, focusing on error detection and correction. This is where I learned the adage, "garbage in, garbage out." We learned how to inspect incoming data and deal with unexpected input. This was mentioned repeatedly by the professor as computers were not forgiving. Programs should follow the 80-20 rule: 80% error checking and repair code and 20% processing logic. To this day, I believe modern programmers have never been taught this lesson.

So, we all worked on our program over the course of the semester. We each created a deck of cards containing data to be input into the program. We each perfected our program using our test data making sure the program worked properly.

On the last day of class, our professor asked us to turn in our program which he would execute. He took each of our test data decks and then did the unimaginable—he shuffled them like a deck of playing cards. We all gasped! Many of us wrote our programs to expect input data in a specific order and format and realized our programs would fail. Thank goodness, I paid attention to what we were taught in class. My program was the only one that worked properly.

During my senior year, I was approached by a graduate student named Bernie. (Several years later, Bernie recruited me to work with him at ROCOR as their systems programmer.) He had written a stock market simulator for an economics professor and asked if I would take over for him since he was nearing the completion of his studies. You guessed it, I said yes and was introduced to the professor the next day. I'm probably the only student to take an upper division economics course and never step foot in the classroom. Another A.

Toward the end of the semester with graduation approaching, I noticed a job posting on the department's bulletin board. It said that if CS majors were interested in a non-defense (the Vietnam war was raging), well-paying programming job to see the chairman of the department, Professor James Haag. I subsequently interviewed with the San Francisco Unified School District and got the job. I still have that bulletin board posting.

I will always be indebted to Ernie of El Paso Texas for kindling my passion. As the expression goes, if you love what you are doing, you will never work a day in your life.

The IBM 1130 computer with a portion of a keypunch machine to the right.
Photograph courtesy of Wikipedia.

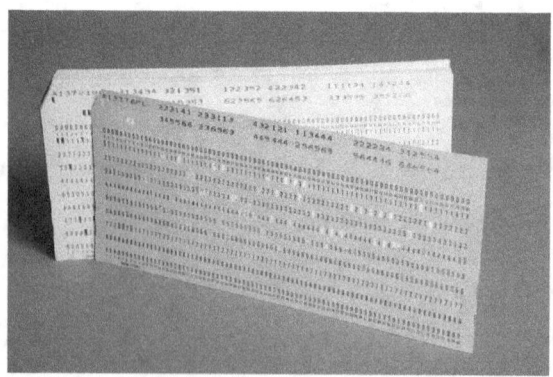

Deck of computer punch cards.
Each card can hold as many as eighty characters.
They are created by using a keypunch machine.
Photograph courtesy of Wikipedia.

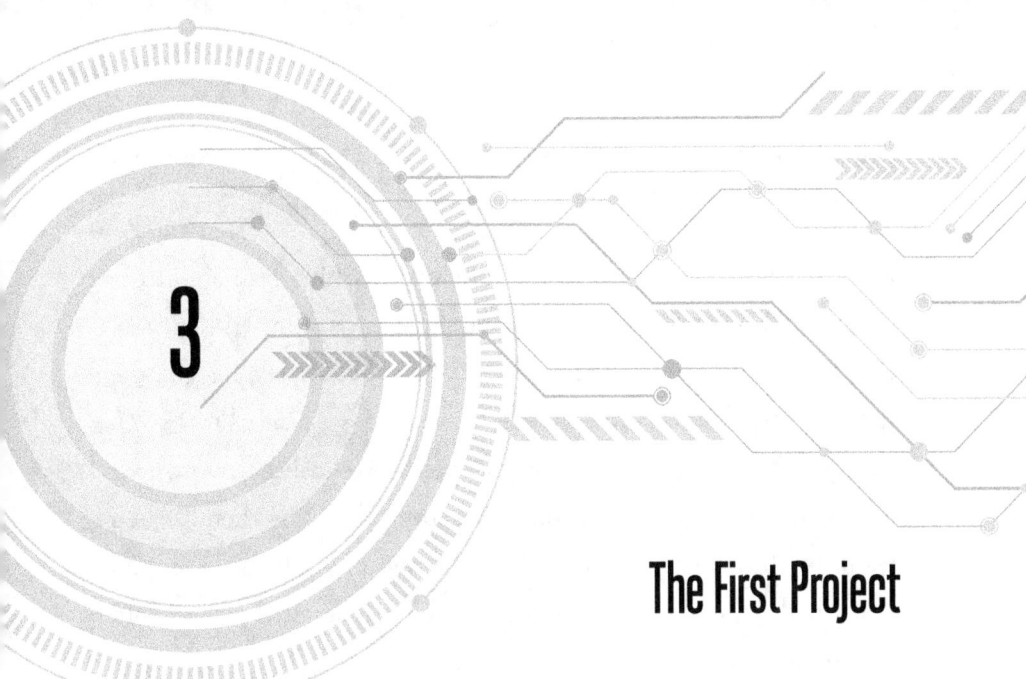

The First Project

My first job began in 1972 as a programmer/analyst with the San Francisco Unified School District which I started immediately after graduating. As a new hire, most of my time was spent learning a programming language, PL/1, which was used by SFUSD. I was given some minor programming tasks such as performing maintenance (e.g., bug fixes, changes in report formats, etc.) on existing programs. While not overly exciting, it was an excellent way to learn my new craft. This went on for just about a year. I kept regular hours and enjoyed the work very much.

It turned out I had a gift for fixing "bugs" in computer programs. I was asked to look at four programs written in an extremely cryptic language called RPG that were not working properly. It was going to be a struggle since I had never used RPG before. As a first step, I decided to meet with the person for whom the reports were being produced. Hopefully he could tell me what the correct result should be and then I could figure out how to fix them.

I will never forget going into his office and asking him about the reports. He smiled and then pointed to a two-foot-tall stack of green bar computer paper in the corner. Whenever he got the reports from Data Processing (that's what IT was called in 1972), he just tossed them on the top of the stack—in other words, he never used them and never told us to stop producing them! When I told my boss I was finished with the assignment, he was stunned that I had done it in less than a day. We both laughed when I told him the whole story.

The shop used an old IBM 360/50 mainframe for which we used punch cards to communicate with it. When we wrote a program, it was transferred to punch cards via a keypunch machine, one line per card. All programs were run in "batch mode" meaning the programs were run one at a time by the computer operator. During days of heavy production, you might only get one or two runs all day.

IBM 360/50 mainframe computer in a typical computer room configuration. Photograph courtesy of IBM Corporation.

One of my next assignments was to perform maintenance on a payroll program. The task was to update teacher payroll withholding percentages. It seemed simple enough, and I proudly submitted the updated program to production. About a week later, I was called into the Data Processing manager's office. He asked me if I changed withholding rates in a certain program. I told him I did. Well, it turns out something went wrong, and the program incorrectly paid every teacher in the San Francisco Unified School District. Fortunately, it was a small amount, but nevertheless, the teachers were not amused, and hundreds called in to report the error. Well, I figured I was about to get fired in my first month on the job. He asked me if I tested the program and asked me to bring in my test results. It turned out my test only looked at a small sample of teacher records and ignored the rest. The manager told me to take a deep breath and relax. He said that every programmer makes a big mistake sometime in their career, and I had just made mine. Wise words. From that moment forward, I tested the heck out of all my programs.

> *IMPORTANT TIP: No matter how sure you are of your work, test, test, test, test. Better yet, have someone else test it for you. Always remember the 80/20 rule.*

One day in May, the programming staff was called into a meeting by the IT manager. Len told us we had an opportunity to replace our mainframe with a new state-of-the-art model, obtain a new database management system (DBMS), online software (instead of batch), and CRT terminals. This was "music to our ears" as we all longed for this new technology. It would be paid for by a grant from the federal government to help San Francisco integrate their schools. All we would need to do was design, write, and implement an online attendance tracking system that would run on terminals in all 120+ schools. The only "catch" was that it had to be done before the start of school in September.

We all knew this would mean extremely long hours, involving night and weekend work. Len asked us if we were up for the challenge. If we took on the project, there would be no stopping, no turning back, no one else to help us. A no vote would mean we would be stuck in batch mode for gosh knows how long. Well, it took this young group only moments to give a resounding yes to Len and then we returned to our offices to ponder what we had done to ourselves.

The project started with the arrival of several boxes of manuals, and we all dug in, trying to learn the new software. The bad news was that we could not do any programming since our 360/50 was not capable of running it. Our new mainframe would not be delivered for two months, so IBM said they would give us time on one of theirs in their downtown customer data center. I volunteered to help Al, our systems programmer, who had the task of setting up the operating system. We obtained six IBM 3340 disk packs that we transported along with decks of cards and reels of magnetic tape to IBM once or twice a week in the evening and attached them to the 370 IBM mainframe. We installed the operating system on the main disk pack, created the supervisor program (called the SYSGEN process), and installed a myriad of software tools that we would need. At the end of each night, we packed everything up and took it back to our office.

This work went on for several weeks, culminating with the installation of the DBMS system and creation of the databases we were going to use. It was a lot of work, and I enjoyed every second of it.

While Al and I focused on creating the system, contractors were busy in our computer room preparing for our new mainframe. Water-cooled air conditioners were installed after being hoisted by crane up 3 floors and brought in through a window. Large 4" copper pipes connected the air conditioners to cooling equipment on the roof. Additional electrical panels and conduits came next, followed by the installation of an 18" high raised floor which would cover up all the pipes, conduits, new power outlets, end eventually a myriad of what IBM calls "bus and tag" cables that would connect the mainframe to its peripheral equipment (card reader, printer, disk drives, tape drives, console, telecom controllers, etc.)

The day finally came when the new mainframe arrived. It was so large, it wouldn't fit in the elevator. They removed one of the large windows in the computer room and used a crane to hoist the computer up to the third floor. Lots of tense moments as they wrestled the computer through the window opening and onto the raised floor. While all this was happening, we did a final backup of all the data on the old disk drives. Then the 360/50 was powered down for the last time, uncabled and removed along with its peripherals. I removed the heavy rectangular aluminum plate that was on the top of the mainframe, showing its model number. (I still have it to this day.) Then the new mainframe was brought in and placed on the new floor. A small army of IBM Field Engineers (FEs) took over installing all the new equipment and connecting the 2" thick bus and tag cables. A minor setback occurred one day when one of the solder joints on the 4" copper water pipes came apart and partially flooded the computer room. Fortunately, there was no damage to the new computer, thanks to the new raised floor.

Now the hard work began. We first had to reinstall and test all our existing programs. Data had to be loaded from backup tapes to the new disk packs. Bugs that surfaced had to be fixed, programs recompiled and retested. The operations staff had to learn how to operate the new computer. Dedicated high-speed telephone lines had to be run to all the schools along with modems and two IBM 3270 CRT terminals installed.

Getting these lines to operate properly was a major challenge. The lines were composed of multiple circuits daisy-chained between phone company offices and terminating at the school. There was always at least one segment that did not work. I recall one day I organized a conference call with each telephone company office, myself in the computer room, and IBM FEs in the schools. We started testing the line going from the computer room to the first telco office, then we tested the next, and so on. Everything was going well until 10 am when all the telephone techs stopped working—it was their break time! Restarting the testing process was excruciating as many of the techs were replacements and needed to be brought up to speed. It was not until later that we learned our network was breaking new ground with Pacific Bell.

Once the new 370/145 and the phone lines stabilized, my focus shifted to designing and programming the new system. Learning the new Cincom System's TOTAL® DBMS and the online terminal system, IBM CICS/VS, was exceedingly difficult. If it were not for the help of an IBM engineer who was assisting us, we would never have completed the work.

I do not recall how many new programs we had to design, write, and test, but it was a huge number. We got into a routine of working until about 11 pm every night. Some of our families took turns bringing us dinner, particularly Al's wife, Sharon. There were also a lot of Chinese food, pizza, burgers, casseroles, and coffee. This went on for the better part of two months. The looming September 1st deadline was never out of our thoughts.

I was asked to focus on preparing the new databases. I had to write programs that transferred the existing school data, including student records, from the old flat batch files on magnetic tape to TOTAL. Every night I loaded several school databases and finished the evening by sending a memo to Len summarizing the evening's work. When the 120+ databases had been loaded, Len gave me a written commendation emphasizing how important and useful my nightly recaps were to him.

IMPORTANT STRATEGY: IT folks often focus on doing their technical work but fail in keeping colleagues and management informed of their progress, issues, schedules etc. Do not underestimate the importance of personal communications. Status reports, PowerPoint presentations, staff meetings, emails, etc. are essential and can make the difference between a satisfactory worker and a star performer.

We worked on our programs up to and including the first day of school. The primary application was attendance where school staff would use a light pen and CRT terminal to indicate which children attended school that day. This was very important as the school district's funding was based on how many students attended school each day.

Thanks to everyone's hard work, everything went very smoothly. Yes, some bugs surfaced, but fortunately they were only minor. The phone lines continued to cause problems, but by this time, my rapport with a senior PacBell tech went a long way to getting things fixed.

One of our schools reported a daily problem with their terminals. Every day at precisely 10:02 am, their terminals would go down and stay down the rest of the day. Repeated trips to the site failed to solve the problem. We replaced both terminals and the modem at least twice! The finger pointing between IBM, PacBell, school staff, and us was unrelenting! Someone finally asked what happened at 10:02, then it occurred to us—recess started at 10am. What do students do at recess? Many go to the restroom. When the first toilet was flushed, the terminals would go down! Turns out the terminals and modem were plugged into an outlet with a ground wire connected to the cold-water pipe of a restroom toilet. The connection had come loose, so all it took was the jarring of the pipe caused by a flush to break the circuit.

After a short while, things became routine, and we began celebrating our success. It was a great day when Len passed out overtime checks and granted much needed vacation time. I didn't realize I was also eligible for comp time. I wound up taking more than a month off with pay.

Shortly thereafter, I was promoted to senior programmer/analyst after obtaining the highest score on San Francisco's Civil Service exam. I realized my interest was shifting from application programming to systems programming and networking. About a year later, my third year on the job, I was promoted to operations manager and had a staff of twenty keypunch operators, control clerks, and computer operators. I was required to take a civil service oral exam to finalize the promotion. I was told I was not eligible for the position since I did not have five years of experience. I filed an appeal stating I had a computer science degree from a 4-year university and had held jobs as a teaching assistant, staff programmer, and student computer operator. Surely this would make up for not having the five years of operations experience. Well, the Civil Service Commission agreed that they would count my time as a student computer operator as experience so I could have the job, however, at my old senior programmer/analyst salary for two years. I left SFUSD shortly thereafter.

Looking back, I consider working at SFUSD the perfect job to begin my career. I made many new friends, learned many new technical skills, learned the value of hard work, and most importantly, realized you can accomplish seemingly impossible tasks if you put your mind to it! I also learned Civil Service does not reward hard work and skills but only time on the job. No wonder our governments are in such sad shape.

Little did I know at the time the desegregation/integration project was the first of several major projects I would encounter during my professional career.

4

Prepare For The Unexpected

I remember seeing the poster, "To err is human, but it takes a computer to really mess things up." You have already read about my first experience making a big mistake. Of course, mistakes happen in all walks of life, but what makes IT unique is the magnitude of the impact they can have. If data is lost, the result can be catastrophic to a business.

Possibly more damaging than lost data is when data gets contaminated. This usually happens when a program makes an erroneous change to all the records in a customer database, an accounting system, or some other file. I recall one failure at a bank where they miscalculated the interest due on several million customer savings accounts. It took months to correct the damage and soothe angry depositors and regulators.

The primary protection against software failure is rigorous testing. Several books have been written on testing techniques. Each programming shop has its own policies and procedures for testing, and it is imperative they be followed.

At some point, every company will experience some sort of data loss or contamination. Once that happens, companies rely on their backup systems. Backups are simply copies of the data kept separate from the live data. They can take many forms, most common being a full copy of the data put on another disk, computer tape, or other storage media. It sounds simple enough, but it's not. Decisions need to be made on how to do the backups, what media to use, how long to keep them, and how to use them once a failure occurs.

As you will read below, the biggest issue with backups is that companies are lulled into a false sense of complacency. They believe their backups are good, but once a bad thing happens, they find out they are not useable. The reason for this is that they are not tested. It's easy to make one, but much harder to test them. A lot of computer and manpower resources are consumed making backups, but some IT managers consider them boring and of little value. In actuality, it is hard to simulate a system outage and then go through the retore process to ensure the backups are reliable. There is a risk the backup data will write over production data compounding the problem.

> *IMPORTANT TIP: there are only two types of data in the world: data that has been backed up, and data you are going to lose! Backups are applicable to individuals as well. Have you backed up the contents of your laptop and cell phone recently?*

For those of us that work at home, backing up our home devices can often be overlooked. While we are in the office, we rely on the IT department to protect our work, but what about at home? Fortunately, there are a number of things we can do to protect our collections of music, photographs, and the "great American novel" we are writing. For a small annual fee, home users can subscribe to a cloud backup service. An app watches over your PC and automatically copies your work via the Internet to their data center. If your laptop breaks, is stolen, damaged, or you accidentally erase something, you can use the service to recover it.

Many years ago, before it became commonplace to work at home, I found myself writing a technical paper for my employer in my home office. I spent days working on this paper and when it was finished, I decided to make a copy of the diskette. I took the diskette out of the PC's drive and before I could insert it into another drive for copying, I dropped it. Normally not a big deal except for the fact, my 10-week-old puppy who was sleeping under my chair grabbed the diskette and put about a dozen holes in it with its sharp puppy teeth. It was at this point I became a lifelong advocate for backups.

No discussion of backups is complete without talking about disaster recovery. Once backups are in place and tested, well-managed companies will shift their focus to the topic of disaster recovery. Disasters can be caused by fires, earthquakes, floods, hurricanes, terrorist attacks, and so on. Typically, when a disaster of this magnitude occurs, backups are of no use as they too were destroyed along with servers, network equipment, paper records, buildings, etc. Companies must put measures in place to restore company operations. The cost to recover can be extremely high, so many companies simply ignore it and count on good luck to protect them.

In 1975, I was recruited by Bernie (remember Bernie at USF?) to work at his company, ROCOR International. ROCOR was a nationwide trucking company headquartered in Palo Alto, California. I was going to be their Systems Programmer, responsible for maintaining the DOS/VS™ operating system of their mainframe computer, an IBM 370/135. During the interview process, I learned their systems programmer was fired months ago for being drunk on the job on multiple occasions. I learned later ROCOR had been without a systems programmer for almost a year.

I had given my two weeks' notice to SFUSD and was looking forward to a new job. Shortly thereafter, I received a call from Bernie saying their entire computer system was down, and the company could not load or unload a single truck. Apparently, their main system disk called the SYSRES disk pack failed causing the mainframe to crash. They tried to create a new one using backup tapes, but they were incomplete. They had been performing backups every shift but never tested them. He asked if I could come down immediately to help. After getting Len's approval, I went to Palo Alto.

When I arrived at their datacenter, I saw the owner of the company in the operations manager's office yelling at him, Bernie, and the IT director. The company would be out of business in less than a week if service could not be restored quickly. ROCOR used a homemade telecom system that communicated with teletype terminals in all of their offices throughout the country. While it was down, the entire trucking operation came to a screeching halt. It was not lost on these three men that the future of their company now depended on a 25-year-old stranger.

Bernie took me to the former systems programmer's office where we discussed what needed to be done. A whole new SYSRES pack needed to be created and fast. I asked Bernie for the latest operating system tape from IBM, thinking he would simply give me the latest one to get started. He then pointed to a 3-foot-tall pile of tapes in the corner of the office and said it was somewhere in the stack. For almost a year, whenever they received a tape from IBM, they just threw it on the pile.

After what seemed like an eternity searching through the pile, I found the tape I needed. I quickly prepared a card deck containing the commands to load the tape to a new disk pack and initialize a basic SYSGEN process. I took it to the computer room, introduced myself to the computer operator, and told him to run the deck, which he did. Since this process would take several hours, I went back to what was now my office and began preparing a card deck of commands that would be needed to make a functional operating system. I also sorted all the tapes by content and date to make finding additional tapes easier.

As soon as the SYSGEN process created a new OS, I issued a series of commands to find out what was on each of the remaining seven disk packs with the hope of finding their program library. The executable program library had been lost, but fortunately, I found their source code library which contained hundreds of programs. Bernie told me the names of the programs that comprised their homemade telecom system which communicated with devices in all their truck terminals. I started recompiling them and putting them in a new executable library. Again, several hours went by, but finally I was able to get the telecom system operational. The recovery was far from complete but at least the trucks could move again.

After being there for more than twenty-four hours, I went back to my home in San Francisco for some much-needed sleep. I returned to ROCOR shortly thereafter and focused on getting the rest of their programs functional. This turned out to be quite an effort as many bugs that had surfaced months earlier surfaced again. I discovered the old system programmer applied many bug fixes to the OS, and of course, documented none of them. Since we were starting from the beginning, all those bug fixes were gone. I had to research each one, find the fix in the pile of tape reels, reapply it, then recompile and test the program. This effort ultimately took weeks of work.

Now that function had been restored, I did a complete backup of the SYSRES pack, and headed back home. I finished my final two weeks at SFUSD and officially started work as an employee of ROCOR. The company was so thankful, they gave me a raise on my first day.

It was during my first week when Bernie invited me to the corporate office to meet everyone. Walking into the office, I noticed a picture of my father hanging on a wall. I knew my father worked for a trucking company called ONC Freight Systems when I was a child. ONC was owned by ROCOR. The owner knew my father and immediately thereafter I wasn't known as Mike or Michael, but Pete's kid.

I stayed at ROCOR for about eighteen months. During that time, I instituted a process where changes to the SYSRES pack were backed up every shift. I changed my work week to Sunday to Thursday. I would come in on Sundays when the company was closed to do a full backup of SYSRES and the other disks. I then put the new backup disk in production, ensuring it was good and set the old SYSRES aside. On Sundays, I also performed system maintenance: O/S patches, software fixes, new software releases, etc.

I also created what was known as the "Red Binder" for operations. I documented procedures for the computer operators to perform in case something went wrong. For example, if the console broke down, there were instructions for issuing operator commands via the card reader. If the printer broke down, output could be redirected to magnetic tape for printing later. I remember being awakened in the middle of night by an operator telling me the console broke down and the Red Binder worked perfectly. I had no trouble falling back to sleep.

There was a nationwide Teamsters strike in 1976 that lasted almost a month. It took a toll on many companies, including ROCOR. Sensing the inevitable, I secured the services of a recruiter and accepted an offer at Bank of America in San Francisco. I attribute my ROCOR experience and the Red Binder for getting a job at the world's largest bank.

IMPORTANT TIP: Never trust your backups. Most company executives, including some CIOs, don't want the disruption or added expense. As it would turn out, many of the companies I would later work for had inoperative backups and did not know it. Later, it became a standing joke in the Leonardich household that whenever I started a new job, something was going to break and there would be no usable backups.

5

Problems and Opportunities

Every business has its share of problems and opportunities. Just ask any business owner or CEO how difficult it is to stay in business. Companies that do not address their problems or capitalize on their opportunities will not last long. Some you can defer action; others require immediate attention.

Besides delivering a product or a service, owners must constantly strive to be as efficient as possible and protect resources against waste, misuse, theft, damage, and other maladies. Controls must be put in place to prevent problems from occurring. They take many forms and can be both people oriented or technology oriented. Examples include requiring two people to sign checks, expense reports needing manager signatures, multiple layers of passwords on vital systems, changing passwords frequently, and the list goes on and on.

Even the United States federal government mandates certain financial controls for public companies and hold company board of directors accountable if they don't ensure the books are accurate. The following life experience shows the lengths to which one company went to establish controls over their applications.

My position at Bank of America was in the data center operations division in a seven-story building at the corner of Market and Van Ness in San Francisco. (Coincidentally, this location was one block away from the San Francisco Unified School District.) This was the bank's only datacenter serving all its branches throughout California. It was chock full of the largest IBM mainframes, disk drives, printers, check sorters, an internal mail processing facility, and a huge cash vault.

Every night, after the branches closed, couriers would pick up checks, deposit and withdrawal slips and other items and take them to the building. The bank operated a good-sized fleet of trucks and airplanes to service far away branches. The volume of materials and number of branches resulted in an operation that was equivalent to processing the mail of a town of 40,000 people. On a busy night, about eight million checks would be processed. Throughout the swing and graveyard shifts, all this material would be read by the giant check processing machines, sorted, and then sent down to the mail room to be returned to the branches before the start of the next business day. The mainframe computers would post all the information to customer accounts, print statements, apply interest payments, etc. Time was of the essence as all the work needed to be done by 6:00 a.m. in order to make courier deadlines.

The bank had a deep and dark secret at this time. There were about a thousand programmers writing and maintaining all the bank's applications. A programmer would put his/her program on a deck of punched cards, then take it up to the main computer room and hand it to an operator who would then run it. There were absolutely no controls or quality assurance measures. The operation was experiencing a high application failure rate, and nightly program failures were the norm. On many occasions, the problems would be so severe, the courier deadlines would be missed thereby impacting branch operations.

Management knew something had to be done so they decided to start a quality assurance function, and I was the first person they hired for the group. It took us about a year to develop a series of written procedures for making changes to production. I was appointed manager of the new QA group.

We had a process for regular changes, emergency changes, and special processing requests. These procedures called for the programmers to provide evidence of successful testing along with their card decks.

The programmers were banned from the computer room. Instead, they submitted their card decks to the QA group along with test results and documentation. QA analysts would review each change and either send it to operations or return it to the programmer for repair. Operations loved these new processes and program success times almost instantly went from 60% to 90%.

Of course, the programmers and their management hated the new procedures and fought their implementation viciously. I cannot begin to describe the number of meetings I attended that included shouting matches between programming vice presidents and the operations VP.

Besides checking the programs and documentation, my QA group implemented a procedure whereby we would take the programmer's card decks and run them in test mode to catch any errors. We would take them to the computer room, surround them with special Job Control Language (JCL) and have the operators run them. We would review the results and either approve the change to be implemented or return it to the programmers for repair. The rate of successful changes climbed to 95%+.

Every morning, I represented the QA group at an operations briefing held at 8:00 a.m. It was presided over by the EVP of operations, and every group was represented. We reviewed how the evening's work went, problems that occurred, etc. Some meetings lasted 10 minutes, others much longer.

The meeting always started with a report from the mail room indicating if the couriers made it out the door on time. I will never forget one meeting when the mail room person said they missed the courier deadlines. When the EVP asked why, he stood up, pointed to me and said, "…He did it." It turns out one of our JCL test decks had a misplaced command in it. At the end of the test, our test deck would delete all the test files that had been created during the test. There was one deck where the erase command was misplaced, and it erased the entire SYSRES pack. All programs were gone, and the datacenter crashed hard! It took hours for technicians to restore the SYSRES from backups and restart production.

The EVP was not amused. My boss and I spent quite a bit of time in his office, and I felt my career would be coming to a quick end. Frightening to realize a single punched card with a '/*' on it brought down the entire bank. Fast forwarding, this incident resulted in the creation of a separate test facility for the bank complete with its own mainframes for use by the programmers and the QA group. Once it became operational, the successful change control rate rose to 99%.

As a result of this success, the head of operations called me into his office and offered me a new position, which would be a promotion. They were starting up a new line of business that would have its own mainframes and needed someone to manage the operation. The difficult part was that it would be a swing shift job. After much thought, I declined the offer. Being a young person in San Francisco, I enjoyed an active social life and did not want to give that up. Looking back, that may not have been the best decision I ever made as this new business line was something called BankAmericard™ which would eventually be VISA™.

I subsequently found myself in a management grooming spot, working for John, the VP of Systems Programming. It was the bank's practice to assign young "up and comers" to a senior manager to learn the administrative aspects of the operation. When I met the VP for the first time, he said my job was very straightforward. All I had to do was clean up the administration of his one-hundred-fifty-plus-person operation and allow him to go on vacation. He told me things were so bad, he hadn't been able to take a day off for years.

The biggest task I was given was to prepare the unit's $10M+ annual budget. Doesn't seem like much now, but in those days it was huge. It entailed lots of analysis of expenditures and forecasting what money would be needed for the upcoming year. It sounds simple enough, but you need to understand budgeting at the world's largest bank was extremely complex requiring months of work and several iterations. I was given two typists to assist me because the budget package was a hand-typed document more than a hundred pages long. Whenever a number changed, a major portion of the package had to be retyped. Thank goodness for correction fluid. The process was excruciating.

During this time, Apple introduced the Apple II computer. Shortly thereafter, the world's first spreadsheet, VISICALC, came on the market. With the approval of my wife, I had already purchased one with assistance from Employee Loan. (The 16K Apple 2, a 12" B&W monitor, and an Epson MX-100 printer cost $3,500.) It took me "two seconds" to realize the budget process could benefit from this technology. I approached the VP about getting an Apple and was told, "We're a mainframe shop. Nothing will come of these toys..." So, I took matters in my own hands and developed a VISICALC spreadsheet at home. It wasn't long before the VP noticed green bar reports on my desk and started paying attention to what I was doing. It was a great day when the VP asked me to change some numbers by going home in the middle of the day to produce a revised spreadsheet, then return to the office.

The budget was finally finished and submitted. The VP came into my office a short time later, shook my hand, and said "his budget" was the only one that had no errors and was accepted by the bank's budget gods! He also gave me a check for $5,000. I was honored to know I was the only administrative person to receive a bonus that year. Oh yes, and I was allowed to buy one of BofA's first PCs.

IMPORTANT TIP: When I brought the first version of the budget to the VP, he asked me if I bet my job it was correct. My body language gave me away and he handed it back to me saying, "Come back when you can." I found some errors which I corrected and went back to the VP. He asked me the same question, "Do you bet your job this is correct?" This time I said YES! He said "Good, because you're betting my job too." I used this approach several times in my managerial career, and it served me very well.

More time passed, and the VP enjoyed his first vacation in years. He promoted me to the manager of MVS Systems Programming, which was a very prestigious position in the bank. (MVS was the name of the IBM operating system running on all of the bank's mainframe computers.) Realizing I knew little about the IBM OS/370 operating system internals, I was sent to Boca Raton for two weeks of training. About half-way through, I realized this was not my "cup of tea" and began giving a great deal of thought about my next career step.

6

Focus on the End User

Throughout the course of my career, I have come into contact with hundreds, if not thousands of IT people. They seem to fall into two broad categories: those that focus on technologies, and those that apply their skills to benefit their company and its end users. The technologists have their place as they are needed to implement and maintain all the hardware and software that comprise the IT function. They comprise the stereotypical IT person. Most of them work in computer or network equipment rooms, or simply stay at their desks digesting the latest vendor manuals and studying for their next certification. They often frequent vendor presentations and trade shows to keep abreast of the latest gadgets.

I firmly believe the second group of IT people are of equal or more value to a company. Let's be honest, technology can be very intimidating to the non-IT person. End users, as they are called, use personal computers or computer terminals to get their work done. End users can be clerks in the Accounts Payable department, administrative assistants, managers, and yes, even company executives.

Learning how to use devices is the easy part, mastering the software applications running on these platforms is much harder. Their plight is complicated by the fact the applications are constantly changing. Particularly challenging are home-grown applications built by in-house IT developers. You can't use a manual or textbook or Google inquiry to answer a question about them.

So, what is an end user to do? They must rely on company help desks and PC technicians for assistance. These folks know the technology, but more importantly, have great people skills that allow them to explain complex topics without intimidating the user. They go out of their way to make sure the end user's inquiry is addressed so they can continue with getting their job done.

I found myself supervising two PC techs in a high-tech firm. Bill was incredibly knowledgeable of all the technologies we used and was called upon to solve the most complex user problems. He had an ego that matched his technical acumen. The other was not as technically skilled but was very personable. He knew everyone's names and frequently stopped by end users just to see how they were doing and ask if there was anything he could do for them. It took him longer to solve problems as compared to the first tech, but eventually he fixed the issue.

I remember vividly calling upon Bill to help me, his boss, with a problem. Bill came over to my desk and told me to get out of my chair so he could work on my PC. After fixing the problem, he got up and said, "It's fixed," and started to leave. When I asked him what was wrong, he said in a very condescending way, "Don't worry about it," and went on his way. The day came when the company fell on hard times, and I was asked to lay off one of the two techs. Can you guess which one I kept?

> *IMPORTANT TIP: When dealing with end users, forget all the techie talk; they just want to know what went wrong and how to prevent it from happening again.*

In one company I worked for, the Accounting Department provided lunch to the entire IT department as a way of saying thanks for all the support they have been given. My home office has a number of plaques and statuettes from end users thanking me for all the outstanding support they have received. I treasure each and every one of them, particularly my "Employee of the Year" award from IVUS Technical Services.

7

Grasp Opportunities

One never knows when a life-changing opportunity will come along, so it is important to keep an open mind and not be afraid of "thinking outside of the box." Not only are new ideas vital to keep companies growing but they keep the job fun.

It was obvious to me Data Processing was about to undergo a massive change to the way the world used computers. No longer would end users have to wait months or years for a programming request to be completed by an elite group of programmers with giant-sized egos. Now they could do it themselves.

I still remember walking into my boss's office and respectfully turning down the promotion he just gave me. He was stunned! He couldn't believe I was turning down such a prestigious and powerful technical position. He still did not believe anything would come of these little machines. So, it was back to the admin position. After all, he liked going on vacation. While in this position, I founded the employee PC Users Club and started publishing a newsletter to PC users/owners in the bank. Our monthly meetings grew in attendance, and I earned a reputation as the bank's PC guy. The most memorable meeting we had showcased portable computers that had just begun hitting the market. Club members brought in their personal PCs and I arranged for some manufacturers to provide demo units. On display was the 24-pound COMPAQ portable (which resembled a portable sewing machine), the Osborne 1 with its 6-inch screen, The TRS-80 101, the Apple II+, and many others. The meeting was standing room only!

A short time later, IBM announced the IBM Personal Computer and they started showing up around the bank. My boss sent me back to Boca Raton, but this time for in-depth training on the IBM PC. I learned how to take the PC apart, put it back together, how to configure the various switches and jumpers on the motherboard, how to troubleshoot and replace faulty components, etc. It was great—I was in heaven.

When I returned to San Francisco, a person named Rick was waiting for me. He said he had a wild and crazy idea and needed my help. Rick worked in the retail portion of the bank and had limited computer knowledge, all self-taught. He had attended the portable PC meeting and became impressed with what they could do.

He reminded me of a program the bank had run many years prior where tellers would go to California grammar schools once a week and collect pennies, nickels, dimes from children and deposit them in the student's savings accounts. My wife Suzanne and I both recall filling out a 3-inch square blue deposit slip and putting it and the money to be deposited into an envelope secured with a piece of string so that it could be used over and over. While the total amount on deposit was not large, over a million prospective BofA customers participated. The program was cancelled after a few years due to the cost involved in administration.

Well, Rick came up with the idea of resurrecting the program but this time using a PC to replace the teller—a small version of the immensely popular ATM. The bank would donate the PC and a printer to the school and a PTA person would supervise and take the deposits to the bank. All he needed was 500 computers, some procedures, and of course, some programs. That's where I came in!

Amazingly, Rick's idea was approved by the bank's senior management, and I was transferred to the retail division. Rick added a third person to the team who knew bank procedures and procured space for us in an East Bay bank office. We must have been the smallest department in the bank.

Over the course of several months, Rick and I wrote the software for what would be called the StudentBanking® system. We selected the Compaq Portable and anxiously awaited the delivery of 500 of them and Okidata printers. It was during final testing of the system I discovered a printing-related bug. No matter what I did, the bug kept reappearing. After writing a number of diagnostic programs to isolate and recreate the problem, I determined there was a hardware incompatibility between the Compaq computer and the Okidata printer. I called our Compaq rep and after some gentle persuasion (e.g., threatening to return our 500 PC's), a team of Compaq engineers from Houston visited me. About a week later, Compaq said they found a hardware issue in their parallel port card. Compaq manufactured new parallel port cards and arranged for technicians to visit every school and replace the board at no cost to us.

The Compaq Portable I computer nicknamed "the luggable." It weighed about twenty-five pounds! Photograph courtesy Wikipedia.

We did a pilot with several local schools and refined our programs and procedures. The schools were extremely cooperative and very much enjoyed the experience. I had the pleasure of going to the schools to train the PTA parents and market the program to the students. They were thrilled with the prospect of having their own account and secret password that no one else had access to. The response to the system was remarkable! Students no longer deposited nickels and dimes in their accounts but dollars—lots of them. The bank was happy, the kids were happy, the parents were happy, and the schools were happy. *PC World* magazine published an article about us in their April 1986 issue.

After the pilot ended, we announced the program to the public. We received both newspaper and TV coverage. The response was overwhelming with BofA corporate receiving hundreds of phone calls from parents who were in the program when they were in school praising the bank for resurrecting school bank days. School principals started calling asking to sign up.

On one memorable day, a principal from a San Francisco school in a poor neighborhood where I had set up StudentBanking called me. He wanted to let me know he turned away one student who wanted to deposit $20 in his new account. The principal said 'no' since the student didn't have shoes! I told him the bank understood his action. A few days later he called again saying the parents of that student visited him and were terribly upset. They insisted the money be deposited as they wanted a better life for their son than they had! We were delighted our program was having such a positive impact on the community.

I remember getting a call from one of our branch managers. He was reviewing student deposits at one of our StudentBanking schools and noticed a student had a balance over $5,000! Surely this was an error in our system. It turned out the young account holder was a member of the local 4H group and raised livestock. She had sold one of her animals at the county fair and deposited the proceeds in her account. We arranged for a bank employee to visit the girl and her parents and suggest she move the money into a more suitable and higher interest paying account.

Shortly after the program was in high gear, Rick was advised of a new federal banking regulation requiring all savings account holders to have Social Security numbers. Oh my! Rick flew to Washington D.C. to see if the government would waive the regulation for our grammar school account holders. They gave him a resounding "no" but did acknowledge the value of the program. They agreed to send a representative to each of our schools and issue Social Security numbers "on the spot" to the young depositors. This was done within a few weeks and once again, everybody was happy.

StudentBanking was extremely satisfying and rewarding for me. After all, how many projects afforded the opportunity to design and write programs, come up with a deployment process, select and buy 500 computers, and market the concept to school principals, PTAs and students. It helped us train PTA volunteers, interact with the community, and not be bogged down with red tape, status reports, or oversight committees. Not bad for three people. It also demonstrated even the world's largest bank had entrepreneurial spirit.

StudentBanking School manual with software and student materials.

Photograph Courtesy Author

8

Roll With The Punches

The phrase "roll with the punches" reminds us that we do not get our way all the time, or perhaps most of the time. This is one of life's lessons that young children have a difficult time grasping, taking years to accept. This, of course, is true in business. We learn to analyze why something didn't go the way we wanted it to, what we need to do differently next time, and then move on.

With StudentBanking running in "high gear," my work was finished, so I returned to the bank's IT department. Specifically, End User Computing. While I was away, the bank made plans to move away from paper and batch processing. I was quickly assigned to a team of five that was tasked to select a personal computer that would be used by all the tellers. The team published a set of specifications for the branch machine, and we set about researching what was available in the marketplace. We visited about a dozen manufacturers and analyzed their offerings. Since the bank would ultimately purchase 27,000 PCs, we were extremely popular.

The team finished our analysis and published our findings along with a recommendation, which was Compaq. One day the team was brought into a conference room where we were thanked for our work. We were then told our recommendation had been rejected as senior management selected a brand-new machine that had yet to be announced. The PC soon known as the IBM PS2 was the bank's choice. Needless to say, we were stunned management had withheld this information from us and excluded us from making the final decision. We pointed out this machine did not meet the requirements they had approved earlier, but that did not matter. The team was told the subject was closed and we were to return to our departments. There was no use in arguing. We did our work and had to move on.

Much later, the worldwide business community rejected the IBM PS2 and their OS/2 operating system. Subsequently, IBM suffered one of its worst financial setbacks in history and exited the PC business, selling it to Lenovo. I felt the team had been vindicated. The bank, however, was stuck with them. Little did I know at that time that I would fall victim to IBM's mighty power once again— more on this later.

With our "tails between our legs," the team was disbanded, and we were all given small PC-related projects to do. I found myself temporarily in charge of the End User Computing department when my boss, Judy Garvin, married and took time off for her honeymoon. One day, I was summoned to her boss's office in San Francisco. The VP got straight to the point. He asked me what I knew about a technology called LANs – Local Area Networks. I told him I had received some training on them and read about them in technical journals. He then told me to drop everything I was doing and become the bank's lead on evaluating a new LAN technology from IBM called Token Ring. I was told to install one as quickly as possible in the End User Computing department and publish an evaluation. The bank might want to use the technology in the branches. I thanked him for the confidence he had in me and said I would get started right away.

"Oh, one more thing," he said. I was to return to my office and in Judy's absence do the paperwork to immediately transfer myself and one other person, Leon, to the Advanced Technologies Department. I was to complete the paperwork and submit it before the end of the day. When I asked him if I had any say in the matter, he said no and that the reason would be divulged later. I was also to keep it confidential. End of meeting. On my way back to my office, I couldn't help but feel hurt that I was not asked about the transfer and that the VP would not tell me what was going on. I did the paperwork as directed.

The following morning, the entire department was ushered into a conference room. At the head of the table was the VP. With a somber look on his face, he announced the whole department was being laid off except for two people. Severance checks were waiting for everyone outside. When asked why this was happening, he said management felt the department overlapped with Advanced Technologies and as a cost savings measure, we were being eliminated. He ended by saying that this included the boss who was on vacation and the VP himself. After the meeting, I asked him if Judy knew, and he said no. I asked him if he would tell her and he said no, citing the fact this was his last day and she wasn't to be back for another week. That task would have to fall on my shoulders. A week later, I called Judy at her home as I did not want her to be blindsided when she came into the office. She figured something was up and before I could explain why I was calling she said, "You're going to tell me my job has been eliminated. Right?" Turns out she was aware of the political struggle between the two departments and knew something was going to happen. She thanked me for telling her and congratulated me for surviving.

Over a course of a few weeks, I designed and installed the LAN and got it working. I was immensely proud of the fact my LAN was operational even before IBM announced it to the marketplace. I became the "Token Ring LAN" expert for the bank and went on to install LANs in several other departments.

An amusing sidebar—the Token Ring LAN used a new kind of wiring called shielded twisted pair. It was much thicker in size than the coax we used to connect our terminals and PC's. I needed to find a location on our floor to install the LAN wiring and hubs. The obvious choice was the existing wiring closet, so I asked the telecom department to send someone over to unlock it and show me the closet. I was surprised to see two techs arrive, one carrying an 8-foot-long wood 2x4. I watched one tech unlock the door and suddenly a mountain of black coax cable came falling out of the closet. I was stunned! Clearly there was no room for my LAN equipment. I thanked the tech and then watched as the other tech used the 2x4 as a lever to push all the cables back into the closet while the first tech closed the door.

It was around this time I was contacted by Gary of the Interop/ Networld Conference organization. They had heard of my success with StudentBanking and LANS and asked if I would be interested in being a speaker at their upcoming annual industry conferences.

Their conferences were extremely popular and well regarded, drawing in excess of 100,000 techies. I couldn't resist. Over the next three years, I wound up speaking to audiences of thousands of techies at Networlds in Boston, Dallas, and Las Vegas. To prepare for the conferences, Networld would fly each of us and our spouse to a nice vacation location. Suzanne and I visited Puerto Rico, Breckinridge Colorado, and Orlando Florida. Great fun.

9

Big Boy Toys

M any people spend their professional lives working indoors. Working inside has its benefits, especially if you live in an area that experiences extremes in weather. The downside is that working indoors can be boring, especially if a long commute is involved. So, when I had the opportunity to work in the transportation industry, I took it. Trucks, trains, planes, and container ships have a lot of appeal.

One day, my phone rang. It was Derek calling. I had worked with Derek in End User Computing at BofA where he was a project manager. I knew he had left the bank but did not know where he went or what he was doing. I discovered he moved to American President Lines in Oakland and headed up their End User Computing Department. He told me he was so impressed with my work with StudentBanking and LANs, he offered me a job as manager of their end user hardware/software unit. He made me the proverbial "offer I couldn't refuse." After considerable thought,

I accepted Derek's offer. I remember to this day walking to my car in the BofA Concord employee parking lot with a cardboard box full of personal items and with tears in my eyes. I had technically grown up at the bank over the past eleven years, and hoped I made the right decision.

> *IMPORTANT TIP: A wise person once said we all have our comfort zones, and mine was at the bank. You only make forward progress by stepping outside of that zone and taking on new challenges.*

My first day at APL was an interesting one—I got to pick my own brand of PC, and I chose a Compaq desktop. Everything went fine with the Compaq except when I tried to print something. None of my printouts came out on the printer located near my office. I finally realized I had the printer name incorrect in my profile, so the problem was solved. About a month later the mailroom staff said they had a big box from Hong Kong for me. You guessed it— that is where all my printouts went!

Derek wasted no time giving me my first assignment. I was to work with the Marine Engineering team and install a LAN on one of APL's large containerships. Marine Engineering was to install the Ethernet cabling in select compartments in the ship and I was to worry about the devices and applications. Based upon my previous success, I selected a Compaq PC to be the server, another to be the email gateway, and several more to serve as crew workstations. The Novell server and gateway were to be located on the bridge and there would be workstations in several areas. The implementation went very well, and for the first time in APL's history a ship captain could send and receive email while at sea.

Somehow Compaq Corporate learned of our project and asked if they could see their equipment in action. The notion of Compaqs on the bridge of a huge oceangoing containership was a PR person's dream. We were told the president and co-founder of Compaq, Rod Canion, would be included. Without hesitation, APL agreed. I was fortunate to be selected as their tour guide.

I recall escorting Rod and his entourage to the port, up the steep gangplank and onto the ship. Needless to say, Rod was extremely impressed when he saw his equipment on the bridge of this massive vessel. His photographer took what seemed like a hundred pictures. Like most people, Rod had never been on a containership, and asked for a tour. He was particularly interested in seeing the engine room. On our way to the engine room, we went through a hatch and saw a huge, 16-cylinder diesel engine similar to that used in locomotives. Rod stopped, took more pictures, and commented on the size of the motor. We politely waited for him to stop talking and then indicated it wasn't the ship's engine, it is just the starter. We led him through another hatch and there it was, a 4-story tall, massive diesel engine that was over a hundred feet long. Now, that was an engine! We made a final stop in the engine control room to take more pictures of a Compaq workstation sitting atop one of the consoles.

I never got to hear of the results of Rod's visit, but I am certain Compaq's Board of Directors heard all about it. A year later, when I visited Compaq Corporate in Houston, I noticed a photo of Rod standing next to a Compaq on the bridge of the ship.

American President Lines Container Ship.

Photograph courtesy Wikipedia.

10

Play Nice

One characteristic of the IT profession is that IT folks are well known for spending huge sums of money. Servers, network equipment, data centers, wiring, circuits, etc. can be very expensive. Buying a laptop is one thing—buying a million-dollar mainframe computer or constructing a corporate data center is another.

Everyone knows businesses exist to make money. The more goods and services they sell, the more money they make. Marketing and sales organizations exist to promote company products. Sales professionals are always on the lookout for an opportunity to make the next "big deal" and earn a nice bonus that will come along with it. Unfortunately, there are some that will take extreme and potentially illegal measures to win business over competitors.

I am certain everyone has seen a freight container at some point. It is hard to miss a 40-foot-long steel box being pulled by a truck on the freeway or on a train making its way across country. It is a logistical nightmare for transportation companies to keep track of the thousands of containers in their facilities. Yard operators have to somehow accept hundreds of containers prior to a ship's sailing and put them in temporary parking spaces. When the ship arrives, hundreds more have to get offloaded by giant cranes and moved by a small army of trucks driven by longshoremen to spaces in the container yard. Keep in mind these yards can be hundreds of acres in size and hold thousands of containers. It was an all-too-common occurrence of a container being misplaced, typically by a trucker moving it to the wrong parking space, which resulted in a ship being delayed or an angry customer wanting their perishable freight.

APL came up with the idea of attaching RFID (Radio Frequency Identification) transponders on containers and trailers. These transponders were clever devices—when they detected a particular radio signal, they would reflect it back after adding information such as a container or serial number. Yard operators would use a truck mounted computer to roam up and down all the parking lanes in the container yard to take inventory. A transponder would be buried in the ground at the front of each parking space so the computer could determine where a container was parked. It had the potential to revolutionize the container shipping industry.

> *INTERESTING FACT: Commuters traveling over bridges or via tollways probably have a device in their car identifying them when they travel through toll booths. These too are transponders. San Francisco bay area residents know them as Fastrack®.*

Here is where I came in. I was asked to come up with a technical solution for the vehicle mounted computer system. At that time, microcomputers did not have the computing power to handle this task, so a minicomputer solution was called for. My team and I put together a detailed set of requirements and issued an RFP (Request for Proposal) to minicomputer vendors including IBM, Digital Equipment Corporation (DEC), and others. It called for not only a rugged computer that could withstand container yard chaos but also programming tools we could use to build the applications that would run on the minicomputers.

The responses began coming in. Only one vendor, Digital Equipment Corporation (DEC), seemed to have what we needed. All the others did not meet the requirements identified in the RFP. A short while after the vendors were notified of our decision, I was sitting in my office and, without prior notice, APL's IBM sales rep entered with another gentleman unknown to me. The rep told me they were disappointed with my decision and that I should reconsider their solution. I reiterated IBM did not meet the requirements. They did not offer a minicomputer solution, but merely a PS2 desktop computer with a special ASIC (Application Specific Integrated Circuit) board in it. Making matters worse, the board could only be programmed with Assembler language and not a high-level language such as Fortran, PL/I, COBOL, etc., that our programmers could use.

Once again, the rep strongly recommended I reconsider. When I said no, he then informed me his associate was an IBM lawyer. The lawyer proceeded to tell me if we did not accept their solution, they would take our idea along with the RFID tags we jointly developed with a third party and implement it at their expense in the container yard of our largest competitor up in Seattle. This was outrageous! I thought these "dirty-handed" tactics only happened in movies.

I told them to wait and then immediately went into my boss's office and reiterated what was happening. He immediately took me directly to the president's office and we interrupted him. When I told Bruce Seaton what was happening, he told me to have the IBM gentlemen escorted off the premises and tell them our lawyers would be in touch.

IBM made good on their threat and proceeded with outfitting RFID tags and their technology in our competitor's container yard. A short while later, I learned their pilot failed. Our pilot, using DEC technology, was successful.

Typical container yard with gantry cranes in the background.
Most containers are 40 feet long and weigh as much as 80,000 pounds.

Photograph courtesy Wikipedia.

Shipping container with modern day RFID tag.

Photograph courtesy Wikipedia.

From the day IBM left my office, I have never bought a single piece of IBM hardware or software throughout the remainder of my career. Subsequent employers have asked me to purchase IBM technology, and after recounting my story, they all agreed to accept a different vendor solution. Unfortunately, our RFID solution was cancelled. We had approached the United Nations organization with the intent of securing a single radio frequency that would be used by all trading partners around the world. After months of effort, we could not get consensus, so our system that would revolutionize freight handling was not to be.

Months later, I learned IBM was not the only company that disagreed with my technology choices. It was at this time APL decided to build their own skyscraper in downtown Oakland,

and I was tasked with architecting the data wiring solution for the new building. I published an RFP for the Ethernet hardware and fiberoptic cabling that would be required. After reviewing all the responses, I recommended we accept the solution from a company called Cabletron. Shortly thereafter, I learned one of the other responders, Synoptics, went "over my head" and appealed directly to APL's board of directors. Apparently, I made a good case for Cabletron as Synoptics was also "shown the door."

Baseball fans will undoubtedly remember the October 17, 1989, World Series game between the Oakland Athletics and the San Francisco Giants. It was exactly at 5:04 p.m. Mother Nature decided to unleash some of her fury in the form of a 6.9 earthquake in the San Francisco Bay area. At that very moment, I was standing outside my 21st floor office in the APL building. I had just come out of a meeting with the president of a French software company trying to sell us a million-dollar software system. The building shook violently, knocking over file cabinets and dislodging the contents of shelves. PCs were falling off cubicle shelves, and staff were diving under their desks to avoid getting hit by falling debris. Glancing out my window, I could see brick buildings in downtown Oakland collapsing, flattening cars in the parking lots below.

I grabbed the Frenchman and pulled him into my office where we took cover. When the shaking subsided, we got ourselves up and stood outside my office. The Frenchman said in poor English, "Does this happen often?" One of my wise guy staff members, still under his desk, looked at his watch and said, "Wow, the 4:40 is late today." Well, that did it. The Frenchman "turned white as a sheet" and fainted. I gently lowered him to the floor and contemplated what to do next when he came to and said, "Every day?" So much for his first visit to the USA.

APL was unique in that it allowed Apple PC's to be used as desktops. While Apples were popular with end users, the IT network people would not allow them to be hooked to their mainframe computer and therefore there was no access to email and other services. The Apples were connected to each other via a technology called Appletalk™ which was very slow, but it worked. I soon learned a Silicon Valley company had developed a device called a gateway that would connect Appletalk LANS to IBM SNA networks. I obtained one of these devices and somewhat surreptitiously connected it between the two networks. Apple users were ecstatic. By the time network management found out what had happened, "the cat was out of the bag" and they were unable to disconnect it due to its popularity. As Kelsey Grammar said in the movie *Down Periscope*, "I love this job!"

> *IMPORTANT FACT: The Appletalk network solution used "silver satin" telephone wire and PhoneNet™ connectors manufactured by Farallon Computing. Little did I know I would have a future employer named Netopia which was formerly called Farallon.*

One day, I was summoned to a SVP's office. Roger oversaw all software development at APL and his staff numbered about 150 developers. He asked me if I knew what was different in the way we developed software between the "old days" and today. I replied, "That's simple—we don't use punched cards." He smiled and said I was correct. He offered me a position in his department whose objective would be to reengineer the software development process to make it more efficient.

Since all programmer tools were PC based, I convinced management to buy 100 PCs to equip the staff. My team and I set up file sharing, storage, print services, etc., and began looking at development tools. (Remember the man from France?) All was proceeding nicely until a couple of developers reported hard disk crashes on their machines. Then two more... I had Compaq examine the failed hard disks and discovered the lubricant used in the hard drives seized up after the drive was shut off and it cooled off. We were told to keep the machines powered up until Compaq could arrange to have all the disks replaced.

While we were waiting for the new drives, disaster struck. A motorist collided with a power pole near our office which caused a building-wide power outage. We had an immediate failure of about fifty drives. Realizing all his developers were now idle, Roger contacted Compaq management and arranged for the immediate delivery of 100 drives and several technicians to replace the bad ones. The task was extremely difficult as the programmers had files, including new programs, on the bad drives. Compaq arranged for the services of a disk restoration company to recover the inaccessible data. While it wasn't my fault, I certainly didn't make any new friends in the department.

11

The Best Job and the Worst Job

As you have undoubtedly learned by now, I am not one to be bored at work. In fact, I have been called a workaholic more times than I care to admit to. After APL, I found myself at another Oakland based corporation, Clorox. I was hired to head up their newly formed LAN team in the Network Department and implement LANs in their bleach plants throughout the world. The thought of working at Clorox excited me as not only were they a household name but I figured their IT pockets were dripping with money. After all, bleach is mostly water.

To my surprise, I found Clorox to be behind-the-times technically. They still used Wang technology despite the fact the world had moved on to personal computers and Microsoft applications such as Word and Excel. They just completed building a multi-million-dollar datacenter in Pleasanton. This building was state-of-the-art with raised flooring, redundant power feeds from the local electric company, battery backup, token ring wiring, generators, their own water well for emergency cooling and firefighting, training rooms, and plenty of offices and conference rooms. It was a serious case of overkill as by that time the industry was already moving away from large mainframe computers to minis and LAN servers.

Ray, the CIO, was an avid art lover and saw to it there were original works of art in every room. My office had two paintings, each of which was expertly framed and illuminated by Clorox's art curator. The main conference room had a $20,000 bronze sculpture of a California brown bear. Behind the security guard was a $10,000 art piece about 4 feet by 5 feet in size made of bits of wiring and cabling woven together that were left over from the building's construction. Whenever Ray visited the datacenter, he would inspect (complete with white gloves) the artwork to make sure none of it had been moved.

The director that oversaw the facility seemed preoccupied with everything but technology. My immediate boss, John, was about to celebrate his 25-year anniversary with the company. The director arranged for a lavish dinner party for John and his direct reports and our spouses at the French Laundry restaurant in Napa. I remember he made several trips there to develop the menu and select the wines. The wine list was the primary agenda item at several of his staff meetings.

See where I am going with this? I was glad to know all of Clorox's IT budget was being well spent. I had business dealings with their R&D facility next to the datacenter and soon learned the engineers there looked upon us corporate folks with disdain. Why? Corporate IT had neglected them and provided little or no support. Both IT folks and engineering folks felt their way was the best and refused to consider what the other department had to offer. I gained their respect as I quietly connected their engineering ethernet LAN to the corporate IBM network so they could use email. IT was furious! To this day, Corporate IT probably still doesn't know how that happened.

My first LAN project was to install a network in the Chicago bleach plant. Wiring was nearing completion, and I flew to the plant to observe what had already been done and identify locations for servers and other devices. As luck would have it, I arrived the same day when the city inspector was making his final inspection. I was introduced to him, and he mumbled something like, "The cigar box is in the truck" to me. Since I did not know what that meant, I went about my business. A short while later he came up to me and said we failed the inspection—we would have to put all the low voltage communications cabling in conduit which would add thousands of dollars to the cost of the project. Fortunately, the plant manager overheard and took me aside. He asked me what the inspector said to me and was horrified to learn I ignored what he said. He said he would take care of it. A few minutes later the inspector approved the project and left the facility. I was told the plant manager put a little something in the inspector's cigar box and was told that is how they do business in Chicago.

When I returned to the Bay Area, John gave me a copy of the IBM invoice for the cost of wiring the plant. I was surprised to see a $15,000 amount. I asked John about it and was told they went with IBM since they are the technology leader. After all, they promised to provide as-built diagrams and would provide a lifetime warranty. I politely told him IBM does not do wiring;

they must have used a local subcontractor. Every wiring contractor would provide as-builts and a warranty for wiring is useless as wiring done properly never breaks. I also told him we were being seriously overcharged for a simple and straightforward wiring job. He ignored what I had to say.

Later that day, I went into our IBM rep's office in the datacenter on another matter and stumbled across an invoice from a Chicago wiring contractor. They billed IBM $3,000 for the wiring of the bleach plant! I took this information back to John who seemed stunned. I told John from now on I would manage all wiring installations to which he agreed.

With the wiring done, I turned my attention to specifying the hardware and software that would be needed in the bleach plant: a server, an email gateway, the Novell Netware server operating system, Attachmate email gateway software, and other items. I submitted my list for approval. A couple of hours later, I was told to meet with the CIO in his Oakland office. In front of him was my list. Ray asked me how I developed the list and I told him it was from past experience—all these items had been proven to work well together and were, in fact, running on APL's ships. Ray said this was not acceptable as none of these items were from IBM. I told him IBM did not make these items; all they had was a structured cabling system to run their token ring LAN. He ripped up my list and told me to use only IBM components. I repeated the fact IBM did not make a full LAN solution. So much for trying to rationalize with the boss. He said then I need to work with them to develop what we needed. Surely IBM would listen to us since we were a good IBM customer. After all, we had one of their mainframes. I politely told him IBM would not listen to Clorox as we are a smaller customer, of which IBM probably had hundreds if not thousands. If they wouldn't listen to BofA that had dozens of mainframes including two of the largest ones made (IBM 360/91), they surely wouldn't listen to us. He became furious with me and told me to wait until IBM developed the products we would need.

So, from that day forward, my staff of six and I tried to busy ourselves with other tasks while we waited for IBM to produce what we needed. This turned out to be difficult as there was not much for a LAN group to do who couldn't do LANs. I found myself arriving at the office around 10 am every morning and leaving for home around 3. My wife said it was the best job I ever had since I was home so much. I thought it was the worst due to serious boredom and the fact I saw my company being taken advantage of by IBM and their own backward technology mentality.

So, after less than six months, I left Clorox. A couple months later I read in the newspaper Clorox had a new CEO who wasted no time cleaning house. Ray and all his direct reports in IT were fired for spending too much money and not providing the company with much needed solutions to support the business. Gee, what a surprise!

A week or two later, I was walking down Broadway in Oakland and came face-to-face with Ray. He asked me if I had heard about what happened within Clorox. I told him yes, and I was sorry he had lost his job. He then said "Well, you were right, and I was wrong." I felt vindicated. He then said he hoped our paths would cross sometime in the future, and perhaps I could work for him once again. After all, he had a lot to learn. I said thank you, wished him well, and went on my way thinking to myself that was never going to happen.

12

Impossible Projects

The bulk of the resources in an IT department are devoted to the operations function, that is, keeping things up and running. The remainder of the department is devoted to making enhancements. Some staff are busy writing new software and others deploying new technologies. In 500 BC, the Greek philosopher Heraclitus said there is nothing constant but change which certainly holds true for IT departments. Projects range from the very small to those that seem impossible.

One of the most important facets of any IT department is the corporate network. It is the network that allows the company to communicate with the external world, remote offices, and of course, its employees. The position of Network Manager is held in high regard due to its great level of responsibility. If anything connectivity related goes wrong, the network manager is immediately called upon to fix the problem and restore service as quickly as possible.

After Clorox, I found myself working at DHL in Redwood City. I managed the network department which was comprised of a staff of about 25 voice and data professionals. Most people do not know that DHL was structured similarly to a franchise operation with each DHL division owned by individuals in the country in which the DHL division was operating. The DHL I worked for served North America with approximately 300 locations.

One day I was called into the COO's office and politely told to shut the door behind me. Vic asked me if I was the network manager, which I said I was. He then said he had a high priority project for me. Years earlier, DHL decided to spin off their wide area network and package tracking mainframes. I can only assume this was a cost savings matter. Well, apparently this strategy was not working. The third party was going bankrupt and if that happened DHL would immediately be out of business. The third party was now demanding DHL pay them a million dollars a week to stay in business.

The decision had been made to move away from the third party as quickly as possible and bring the network and package tracking system in-house. It was my job to create a 300-node nationwide telecommunications network as fast as humanly possible. Money was no object. Break all the rules to save the company. I was told to get it done within 30 days! One more thing—I couldn't tell anyone why—should our competitors get wind of this, we would likely be forced out of business in a matter of days.

With that being said, he told me to get started ASAP. I asked him about the package tracking system and he said, the next person he was going to talk to was getting that task. When I left his office,

I noticed Bob, an application manager, waiting his turn to speak with Vic. Bob asked me "What's up?" and I replied "You'll find out soon enough. Hope you're caught up on your sleep."

I returned to my office and immediately started calling telecom carriers, asking if they could install a 300-node X.25 network for us within 30 days. Most politely said no way, with one hanging up on me. Another said yes but would require a signed contract before starting work. When I called Sprint, they told me they had been trying to get DHL's business for years, so yes, they could do it. Feeling a sense of relief, I told them I expected a design team to be in my office the next morning. After that, I broke the news to my staff, and once they picked themselves off the floor, they immediately went to work.

I will spare you, the reader, everything my staff, Sprint, and I went through in the next 30 days. We set up some cots so we could take naps. Sprint technicians were onsite 24 hours a day. We had spouses bring us food and fresh clothes. Some of us did not see our families for days—in fact, there were at least two divorces within the department caused by the project.

We were quite worried the feds would shut down the third party because they had not been paying their payroll taxes. If that happened, we would lose the package tracking capability and we would immediately go out of business. So, taking the COO's direction to heart, Bob and I prepared to break the rules. I rented space in a Sprint datacenter in Alexandria, Virginia near where the third party operated and had Sprint install data circuits to connect to the network. I also rented a moving van. If the doors were padlocked by the feds, we would, in the middle of the night, cut the locks, deinstall the mainframes and move them to Sprint. We put Legal on notice this was our plan and they should be prepared to bail us out if bad things happened. Fortunately, we never had to put that plan into operation.

While we did not make thirty days, we came close. It took us thirty-three. Vic and DHL ownership could not be happier. They invited Bob and me to listen to their phone call to the third party when they announced no more million-dollar checks would be forthcoming and that their services were no longer required.

Interesting to note DHL and Sprint did not complete the contract paperwork for the new network until 60 days later.

Vic scheduled a meeting at Corporate to announce the change. Bob and I were asked to come up to the front of the room. Vic shook our hands, thanked us profusely, and then presented black leather jackets with the DHL logon on the back to both of us. So much for saving the company! While Bob and I expected bonuses for our extraordinary work, that did not happen. We both resigned within the week.

It did not take me long to find a new job. I joined privately-held Marine Terminals which managed deep-water port operations for many steamship companies. While longshoremen loaded and unloaded the ships, Marine Terminals managed the longshoremen and the facilities. They operated facilities in Seattle, Vancouver, Long Beach, San Pedro, Oakland, and New Jersey. It was my job to manage Marine Terminal's sole 24x7 datacenter in Long Beach and the technology in each of the sites. The technology consisted of servers, async terminals, PCs, wide area network lines, LANs, telephone systems, email, and other applications.

I had been on the job only two weeks when I was summoned to the owner's office. Chris told me he had been approached by the world's largest transportation company, Taiwan-based Evergreen, about taking over management of one of their port facilities in Long Beach. This deal had the potential to add $10M in revenue to Marine Terminals, which would effectively double its size. There was a huge "gotcha," however. It had to be done in 30 days, which is when the current stevedore company's contract would end. Chris said I would have full autonomy over the project and a blank check. If we failed, it would most likely result in Marine Terminals going out of business. As they say, "Failure is not an option."

There were a couple of "wrinkles" that would have to be overcome. First, the existing stevedore company would be hostile towards us, and there was a risk of violence. This meant we would not be able to go on to the site until after 5 p.m. on their last day. The second wrinkle was that the first Evergreen ship was scheduled to arrive at 8:00 a.m. the next day! Chris was not making this easy. Fresh off my DHL success, I said I could get it done. I could not help but wonder how I kept getting myself into these seemingly impossible predicaments.

The first order of business was to order a bigger mainframe computer from HP as our current machine would not be able to handle the added load. HP quoted me 6 months! I won't tell you what our rep said when I told him I needed it in 2 weeks. I knew there must be a computer already on the assembly line or on a shipping dock destined for another HP customer. The rep confirmed there was one about to ship to another customer. I persuaded him to call the customer to see if we could "buy their place in line" for a fee, of course. Well, it worked. All it took was a sizeable check.

The second long lead time was to order the custom made fiberoptic cables we would need to connect the eleven buildings on the 250+ acre site together. Since we could not go on the site to take measurements, we dressed two of our employees as longshoremen complete with overalls, orange vests, hard hats, and clipboards. They entered the facility mid-day and paced off the distance between all the buildings. From these rough measurements they drew a site map from which I was able to order the cables. We also ordered the WAN circuits from the phone company that would be used to connect the facility to our datacenter. Thank goodness both were in the same city, otherwise it would have been impossible to get high speed T-1 circuits that fast. We hoped the existing stevedore company would ignore the PacBell techs when they installed the circuits. They had been coached to say they were doing some preventive maintenance.

My staff and I met with the person that would wind up managing the facility and spent considerable time figuring out what equipment we would need: dumb terminals, PCs, servers, LAN concentrators, a telephone system, etc. Orders were placed ASAP. There was a question as to where all this stuff should go. I wound up renting the ballroom at the Long Beach Hilton for a month to be used as our staging area.

I remember Marine Terminal's CFO coming into my office. He told me I was spending money at a rate of about $25,000 per day. He was wondering how long I would be doing that so he could make sure the checkbook was well stocked. I do not recall what I said, but he assured me he would take care of it.

I spent the remaining two weeks working with my team and operations personnel putting together a plan using Microsoft Project. It was excruciating, detailed work but had to be done. That became our bible which we used continuously throughout the project.

I remember sitting in my rental car outside the facility shortly before 5:00 p.m. on the day we were to assume ownership of the facility. It was painful to watch the employees who just lost their jobs walk out with cardboard boxes of their personal possessions and tears in their eyes.

At 5:01 p.m., a small army of technicians I had assembled stormed the facility. I don't recall the exact number, but there must have been at least 30 of us. Our wiring subcontractor showed up wearing a tuxedo. He came directly from a wedding!

We were immediately confronted by our first surprise—the entire facility looked like a junk yard with garbage and old equipment strewn everywhere. We had to use water hoses to wash out the eight small shacks longshoremen would use to check in/out trucks and containers. There were posters of nude women taped to the walls of the breakroom and lunchroom. While ports are not known for being neat and tidy places, if we didn't clean them now, it would never happen. Installing electrified equipment in wet shacks was certainly not for the fainthearted. But there was no time to let them dry.

Halfway through the night came our second surprise. The new facility manager approached me and said he underestimated the number of terminals he needed. We were four short. One of my staff came up with the idea of "borrowing them" from a nearby Marine Terminals customer's facility. We convinced the security guard to let us on the facility, but he did not have keys to the office. Fortunately, someone left a second story window open. Using a forklift, we hoisted someone up to the window. I left a note for the site manager explaining I would replace the four terminals on Monday.

Another surprise—someone told me the team was getting hungry. Yikes, I had failed to realize a hardworking crew would get hungry. The only restaurant open at 3 a.m. in Long Beach was Taco Bell. I'll never forget the manager's face when I ordered a hundred tacos and a hundred burritos and countless soft drinks. It wasn't until I put several hundred-dollar bills on the counter he took me seriously. One team member said it was the best food he had ever tasted. It is amazing how good fast-food tastes if you have been working nonstop for nine hours.

Work continued throughout the night, and fortunately no other surprises surfaced. Since we did not have time to bury the fiber-optic cables between the buildings, we attached them to chain link fencing using cable ties. Another cabling rule broken, but it worked.

One final check at 7:30 a.m. to make sure everything was working. Only 30 minutes until the longshoremen and the ship would arrive. About 10 minutes before 8:00 a.m. we saw the ship approaching the dock and a big black limousine pulling into the facility. It couldn't be any Marine Terminals ownership—Chris was already here. The limo door opens and out walks the Chairman and CEO of Evergreen. He flew over from Taiwan to see his ship being worked by the new stevedore company. After what seemed like an eternity watching the operation, he signaled his approval to the site manager, shook his hand, and left. Fifteen minutes later, all of us who worked throughout the night went to the Long Beach Hilton and drank ourselves into a stupor celebrating our success.

Three months later, Evergreen awarded Marine Terminals with a contract to run their Seattle and New Jersey facilities. Oh, joy—we get to go through all this again. The good news is that for those sites we had entire weekends to get the work done.

Chris could not have been happier. After all, his company tripled in size! He generously rewarded everyone who was involved. Not only did I get a great bonus, but he also recognized the impact the project had on my family. He paid for a week's vacation in Vancouver, BC for Suzanne and me. He also paid for a week for Suzanne, me, and our two sons in Disneyland. That was the first and last time I ever stayed in the Disneyland Hotel, and I enjoyed every minute of it.

It was at Marine Terminals that I became acquainted with an employee named Sid Gerling. Sid's job was to keep the IT equipment running in the ports. He was instrumental in making our Evergreen projects successful, so I transferred him to Seattle to support our port operations there. Sid had always wanted to live in the Pacific Northwest. He is undoubtedly one of the hardest working and most dedicated people I have ever met. One Thanksgiving evening, I was told one of our port facilities was down right in the middle of loading/unloading a ship. I called Sid and found him enjoying Thanksgiving dinner with his family in a restaurant on the top of the Space Needle. Sid didn't hesitate to leave his family and go to the port to get them operational. He was back in time for dessert. Just ask someone to do that in this modern day.

It is amazing what you can accomplish if you "put your mind to it." You don't have to be a genius. All you need is determination, a good plan, an excellent team, and senior management backing.

13

Ho Ho Ho Merry Christmas

As mentioned in the previous chapter, a significant portion of resources are devoted to keeping the operation running. Personnel often work long hours and are on call twenty-four hours a day, seven days a week. Since a lot of what they do entails making changes to the infrastructure, they often work nights and weekends so as not to impact the business.

The Marine Terminals datacenter was in an old building in the port of Long Beach. My predecessor converted a large office into a computer room complete with a raised floor. One day I made the mistake of pulling up a floor tile and discovered a proverbial "rat's nest" of cables, power strips, extension cords, beer cans, and an inch or two of dust and grime. I was appalled. Not only did this make maintaining cables nearly impossible, but it was a definite fire hazard. If the Fire Marshall ever performed an inspection, I was convinced we would be shut down.

I initiated a project to clean up the mess. It turned out to be extremely difficult due to the magnitude of the chaos and the risk of crashing the mainframe or the company network if we pulled out the wrong cable. We did as much as we could, but we soon got to the point where we would have to shut down all the equipment in the room in order to finish the cleanup. Since Marine Terminals' customers operated ships at sea 24 hours a day, 7 days a week, finding a window to cut power was almost impossible. Operations never took a holiday.

It finally occurred to me that there was one holiday that was celebrated around the world—Christmas! I devised a plan to shut the mainframe down early Christmas, reroute its power cables to a panel about 100 feet down the hall using heavy extension cords, restart the mainframe, restore operations, and then work on the cabling. We had electricians put in new power outlets, repair frayed cables, and replace marginal power breakers. Once that was done, we shut the mainframe down, reconnected its power cables to the new outlets, and brought it back up. You can imagine the magnitude of the bill for three electricians working Christmas as well as the overtime for my own staff. It was very difficult being away from my wife and children on Christmas, but it couldn't be helped. Fortunately, my wife was very understanding. After all, she knew she was marrying an infrastructure guy and this wasn't the first time I had to work on a holiday. We celebrated Christmas when I got home the next day. In case you are wondering, we passed our next Fire Marshall inspection.

Don't let this happen to your server room.
It is impossible to replace a bad cable or relocate a user's network connection!
Your Fire Marshall may not be pleased.

Photograph courtesy Wikipedia.

My job at Marine Terminals required me to make day trips to Long Beach once or twice a week to visit the datacenter or one of our container facilities. For those times I had to stay overnight, I stayed at the Long Beach Hilton. I was there so often I was recognized as soon as I walked in the door. "Mr. Leonardich, nice to see you. Your usual room? We'll have Room Service bring up your usual dinner order." It did not take long for me to achieve Hilton Honors diamond status.

This went on for many months. One time I arrived unexpectedly without a reservation. When I walked in, the desk clerk advised me my usual room was occupied. He told me to wait in the bar while they relocated the guests and cleaned the room. I enjoyed the preferential treatment.

It was not two weeks after I left Marine Terminals that the general manager of the hotel called me. Since I had not been there, he was wondering if they did something to offend me and if so, what could he do to rectify the situation. He took the news of my job change and thanked me for my patronage. He said if I ever needed anything to be sure to contact him.

Months later, one of our sons was celebrating a birthday and wanted to go to the Great America Amusement Park in Santa Clara. Since there was a Hilton near the park, I thought we would use some of those Hilton Honors diamond points I had accumulated and stay there for free. I called the hotel and was politely told they had no room available. Drat! Surely there is something that could be done. I decided to see if the Hilton Long Beach manager could help so I called him. He said he would be delighted to assist. Less than an hour later the Santa Clara hotel called and said they had room for us.

A few days later when we arrived at the hotel, the front desk person immediately recognized my name and called the manager. The manager greeted us and said he would escort us to our room. Really? The manager? Leave our bags, they would be taken care of. So, we followed him through a set of locked doors and down a long hallway on the first floor. He explained this wing of the hotel was recently remodeled and not yet open. We arrived at another set of double doors. When the manager opened them, we were greeted with the sight of a huge suite complete with three bedrooms, a big wet bar, several large screen TVs, and every other amenity you could think of. He opened a sliding glass door to a private patio, and there was the hotel's swimming pool right outside our room. He then introduced us to our butler who would take care of us throughout the weekend. Wow! We were overwhelmed. He said this was the least Hilton could do for my past patronage. It was at this point all those long nights away from home didn't seem to matter that much. The suite was so big, we called Suzanne's sister who lived nearby and invited her and her two girls to stay with us. We had a whole wing of the hotel to ourselves.

14

Good News and Bad News

What follows is a rather incredible story of success but with a less than happy ending. I had always hoped to join a company where I could do things my way. A startup? A company that needed a complete IT makeover? Someplace where I could apply all the lessons I have learned throughout my career. The old saying, "be careful for what you wish for; you might get it" summarizes what happened.

Do you recall the name Bob from my DHL days? Bob became the Chief Information Officer of American Protective Services Inc after leaving DHL. APS was the country's largest privately owned security guard company with over 50 locations and 20,000 employees. Their business applications were quite outdated, and Bob was hired to modernize the IT department. The larger branch offices had HP minicomputers and dumb terminals that were used primarily to manage security guard employment records, create work schedules, and do their payroll. The minis would exchange data with the corporate minis on a nightly basis using dialup modems. Everything was batch related as compared to modern real time processing. No email, and few PCs.

So, you probably figured out where this is going. Bob called me while I was at Marine Terminals and asked me to be his IT Director. The prospect of participating in an "IT do-over" and staying out of airports was too good to pass on. I started at APS two weeks later.

The night before my first day, Bob called me to tell me about a company policy he had neglected to mention earlier. APS had a no-beards policy which applied to both security guards and office staff as well. This was quite a surprise as I had been sporting a beard for several years. In fact, my children never knew me without one.

The next morning, I shaved off my beard and saw my face for the first time in at least ten years. I quickly realized I should have shaved the night before as my face was very irritated and looked like a slab of "red meat." I had no choice but to go to work feeling like my face was on fire and I dreaded the first impression I would be making on my new coworkers.

Bob greeted me when I arrived and welcomed me to APS. He escorted me to an empty office next to his, and empty it was. No computer, no telephone, no desk, no chair. I wound up arranging all these items myself and couldn't help but think this was a heck of a way to welcome a new employee. I made a promise to myself that I would never greet a new employee in this manner.

I spent the next month familiarizing myself with my new staff and the technical environment. Bob was right, it was in very poor shape and was holding the company back. What was needed was a complete remake, so Bob and I along with the others got started developing a high-level architecture and "putting some stakes in the ground" to guide our way. One of Bob's stakes was that we were to eliminate all usage of UNIX and the old HP minis in the branches. We also decided to base our new systems on Microsoft Windows, Oracle, Citrix, and a client server architecture.

Enough about technology. Bob and I realized the only way we were going to be successful was by getting the right people. With a high-level architecture in place, we had a pretty good idea of what people resources we would need. Bob put together an organization chart, and I started writing job descriptions. Our HR department was in shock when we presented them with a stack of job descriptions full of technical requirements and experience. After all, they were used to hiring security guards and not accomplished IT people. Over the ensuing months, the org chart slowly got filled in and work to implement the new strategy shifted into "high gear." Since the corporate office was at capacity, there was no room for all of us, so we leased a floor in a building adjacent to the corporate office. There was a never-ending supply of jokes and wisecracks about us by the other corporate folks.

It took about three years to finish the hiring, implement the new technical architecture, write the business applications, install servers and wide area network circuits, and develop and implement a migration plan and get it all working. The business was thrilled. They rewarded us all by giving everyone who was involved with a free cruise to Mexico. Since every aspect of running APS had been changed, there were a lot of folks to reward. Besides IT, there were folks from HR, accounting, insurance, operations, facilities, and other departments involved. The cruises were spread out over several months in order to keep the business running. Oh, lest I forget, the five-figure bonus I received was very much appreciated.

After all the cruises were taken, and business settled into the new routine, an interesting development occurred in IT. After three years of work, many long nights, countless meetings, etc., things got boring. The new systems and technologies proved to be very stable and easy to support. There were no crises! We had put together an incredible, high powered, highly motivated team that did excellent work.

After a short time, we started seeing some resignations as there wasn't enough new work for the staff to do. Bob came up with the idea of using our programming resources to tackle operational business problems. We built several small applications and sold them to our customers. One of the most successful ones was Keytrac, a PC application that customers could use to manage their office/plant/warehouse keys.

We also found ourselves worrying about something called "Y2K." We still had some legacy applications that we needed to upgrade/replace. Due to all the hype in the newspapers and on TV, the business was worried and despite our reassurances, management was quite nervous. To alleviate their fears, we put a team together to work New Years Eve, me included. When midnight occurred, we executed our test plan and assured ourselves and the business everything was working properly. No trouble found!

While APS became a computer savvy company, that didn't apply to everyone. The owner of the company admitted he was afraid of email and therefore did not use it. He wound up making frequent trips from his Tucson home to the Alameda office and undoubtedly had a huge, long distance telephone bill. One day he came into my office to discuss a matter, and I approached the topic of email. I realized his fear was due to a lack of understanding, so I volunteered to teach him email, quietly, of course. A couple of hours later, he was hooked. He loved it so much; he asked if I could send someone to Tucson to set up a PC in his home and teach his wife. Shortly thereafter, the president of APS came into my office. He looked me straight into the eyes and asked, "Did you teach Tom email? I can't get any work done now." Unknowingly, I had created a monster.

Sometime later, all corporate employees were asked to attend a meeting in a nearby hotel. We all crammed into a ballroom where our president announced the company had been sold! The current owner was retiring and none of his children wanted to continue running the business. The new owner was our major competitor headquartered in southern California. It was likely the Oakland campus would be dismantled and we would lose our jobs. Bob and I wasted no time going to their headquarters to meet with their CIO. Surely, she knew of our success and would embrace the work we had done. To our shock, she announced she did not like what we did—too complicated and expensive so the offices would be migrated to their existing systems. We IT folks could either transfer to their office or hit the street. We learned the CIO was a former security officer—no wonder she did not understand the importance of technology to a business. The one-hour plane ride back to Oakland was the longest I have ever taken.

To this day I recall the pain I felt, not just because I was losing my job, but because the top-notch IT department we had put together was going to be dissolved. Yes, I may be prejudiced, but the APS

IT department was the best group of folks I have ever had the pleasure of working with. We were so good, it was as though we could read each other's minds. It was an absolute travesty to see all these talented people who had grown into a successful tightly knit team that felt and acted like family cast out into the cold.

15

Preparation Is Essential

I t takes more than talent and desire to find that dream job. When you get a lead on a new job, you need to research the company thoroughly in preparation for the dreaded interview. You need to determine what benefit you can bring to the company and then sell it. Know who you will be speaking with, what they are expecting, and prepare your answers accordingly. Do your homework. Don't talk generalities, be specific, and don't be afraid to take a risk. As the old adage goes, "No guts, no glory."

After an eighteen-month stint in a DotCom startup called IVUS Technical Services, I joined Netopia, a high-tech communications equipment manufacturer based in Alameda. The hiring manager told me I was her leading candidate and had to be interviewed by the CEO. I found out he was very financially motivated and longed to get a new device called a Blackberry. After all, every CEO had one but him. Their former IT Director told him it would cost $100,000 as their entire email infrastructure would need to be replaced. I investigated Blackberrys and discovered a solution that would not require a full email system replacement.

The day of the interview arrived, and I was ushered into the CEO's private conference room. He took one look at me and said why should he hire me. I could tell he realized I was older than the rest of the IT staff and concerned I did not "know my stuff." I replied he should think of me as a coach of a sports team—the coach was always older than the players since he/she typically had played the sport. While they may no longer be suitable to play, they knew what it took to lead a team and get results.

That didn't seem to satisfy him, so I told Alan I was aware of his desire to get a Blackberry. He responded saying yes, but they are too expensive, so I told him if he hired me, I would get him one within 30 days for about $50 a month. That got his attention! I also said I would cut his company's telecom costs by 40% in the first year. That really got his attention! And if I failed to deliver, he could fire me. That did it. He stood up, said welcome to Netopia, shook my hand and left the room. Total interview time was 15 minutes.

After I started working, he would come into my office two or three times a week for about 10 seconds and drop not-so-subtle comments about Blackberrys and ask when he would get his. Well, I made good on my promise and remember his reaction when I brought him his new device. He was like a "kid in a candy store" and immediately fell in love with the tiny machine. I remember a few days later I got an email from him saying he was in Yankee Stadium and just closed a deal with a new customer. He now achieved parity with his fellow CEOs. He no longer needed to lug his heavy laptop across the country. He kept popping into my office but now it was to tell me how much he liked it and how it had revolutionized the way he did his job. Shortly thereafter, I was told to get them for the rest of his managers and our sales force. Netopia went from one to about two hundred Blackberrys in record time.

16

The Project From Hell

I had been with Netopia about four months when the CEO, Alan, came into my office mid-October and said, "Get your coat. We're going building shopping."

I learned our lease was up on December 31 and Alan had been negotiating with our landlord for months. He had just come from a meeting with the landlord and said that since time was short, Netopia had no choice but to pay his full renewal price. That did it—our CEO became enraged and vowed to move by the end of the year. I won't repeat the expletives that were exchanged by the two men. A hastily assembled team of the CEO, CFO, CIO, facilities manager, and I went to meet with a real estate broker to look at available properties. We must have looked at 6 or more locations, none of which were suitable. We went back to our office and made plans to resume our search the next day. On the ride back, the CEO looked at me and said make the move happen and with no customer down time! We had to move by the end of the year as we would incur a $10,000 per day penalty for every day we were late. This wasn't going to be easy!

Realizing the magnitude of such an undertaking, the first thing I did was to call our PacBell rep and advise her we were moving. Michelle said she would assemble a move team and get back to me in a week. I told her that wouldn't do as we needed to move by the end of the year. She was stunned. Typically, moves of 50,000 square foot high-tech facilities with multiple engineering labs take at least 6 months. I told her to forget the team and I ordered two T-1 high speed lines to connect our existing building to our new building. Michelle said she would put in the order ASAP. All she needed was the address of the new building. When I told her I didn't have it yet, Michelle said I wasn't making this move easy! I told her I need the circuits in two weeks so make up an address and I would change it later.

The next day, we went looking at properties once again. We came across a location in Emeryville that was available. It was two floors in an 8-story building, and the suite we were considering already had a computer room. That was good enough for me, and I recommended we go with it. It turned out the rent was acceptable, so the decision was made. Only one small problem—it was too small. After much discussion and realizing time was short and there were no other suitable locations, the CEO made the decision to take it. We would relocate our engineering lab to our Fremont office that had some vacant space that could be turned into a lab.

The magnitude of such a move cannot be underestimated. Netopia had a computer room full of equipment, a 24x7 technical support call center, multiple engineering labs full of equipment, multiple web sites, high speed circuits to other Netopia locations around the US, and about 300 people—each of which used at least one computer and a PacBell Centrex phone circuit. That meant our existing building had miles of cabling internally and over 300 external phone lines.

I remember holding a staff meeting to break the news to my team. Those involved with the IT infrastructure, particularly my network person and the server person, had expressions on their faces that looked like "deer in the headlights." Thank goodness they were all good folks. We started working immediately. My server person reminded me his wife was pregnant and her delivery date was around Christmas, at which time he would become unavailable. We worked until midnight that first day and came up with a move strategy and high-level task list. Again, a project that wouldn't have time for sleeping.

Further complicating matters was the fact my father, who lived about 125 miles away, had become seriously ill and was in and out of the hospital. I was driving down there frequently to visit him and support my mother. More on this later.

With my staff fully engaged, I turned my attention to designing the floor plan, and in particular, the new lab we would have to construct in our Fremont office. I met with the engineering director and sketched out a design on a napkin for the new lab. It was going to be constructed in vacant space at the back of their office which was currently used for storage. Nothing but a concrete floor, a couple of bare light bulbs hanging from the ceiling and a ping pong table. I already had a relationship with a general contractor in Silicon Valley, so I called him. I told him what I wanted, and after

I said price was no object, he said he could do it—he would send his internal design guy down in the morning. By the end of the next day, we had a semi-detailed design and the contractor would start the next day. The contractor told me it would take about three months just to get the building permits so we took the risk of going without them. Of course, I do not condone doing this, but when your back is up against the wall, you must take drastic measures.

When we were well into the project, my father's condition worsened, and he was again hospitalized. I found myself adopting a routine of visiting Alameda early every morning, going to the Emeryville office late morning, then going to Fremont, then driving down to Salinas at night. I don't remember how long I kept this up, but it was at least two weeks. Thank goodness for my Blackberry. The old joke of catching up on your sleep when you're dead came to mind quite often.

Another problem—we couldn't get cubicle furniture for Emeryville by the end of the year so we had no choice but to use what we had. We came up with a plan to stage the move over three consecutive weekends, moving one-third of the furniture and people at a time. Friday mornings the staff that were moving packed up their cubicles, then the movers came in the afternoon. They disassembled the cubicles and moved them to the new building where they were reassembled Saturday morning. I had a wiring contractor standing by that would wire the cubicles while they were being constructed. The staff's possessions would be moved into the new cubicles Sunday morning, and then we would spend the rest of the day unpacking and hooking up equipment and telephones. It was tightly controlled chaos.

My server person's wife delivered their first baby mid-December, right on time. In order to take up the slack on James' absence, I arranged for my IT person, Ken, located in our Billerica, Massachusetts office to come to California December 1st and stay until the move was completed. It turned out Ken stayed here about 45 days and celebrated a brief Christmas with me and my family. Why brief? We had planned on a Christmas vacation in Canada. My wife and children went without me. Yet another time my family felt the pain incurred by my job.

PacBell called me Christmas Eve to tell me they ran out of cabling going to our new building so they would not be able to provide Centrex phone service to the remaining 110 people that were moving on the third and final weekend. Michelle told me she had already ordered additional cabling and called in a few favors to get it installed Christmas Day. This typically would take PacBell two or three months to complete. I did not press her on how she got the PacBell bureaucracy to move that quickly.

Most of what happened that final week of the year is now a blur. I remember being in Alameda when the last of the moving trucks was being loaded on December 31st and, guess who shows up—it was our old landlord. He was stunned that we made good on our promise to move by the end of the year. Our CEO got great pleasure showing him we had just finished sweeping out the building and handing him his keys.

Early in January the CEO held a meeting for all the staff in Emeryville, thanking them for making the move a reality. Netopia had a special program for recognizing non-manager high achievers every quarter. I had the pleasure of receiving the award—the one and only manager ever to be so recognized. The big bonus check was also very nice.

> *IMPORTANT LESSON: The only way I was able to accomplish such an impossible project was due to an incredibly talented and dedicated team. Netopia is particularly indebted to Michelle of PacBell who worked tirelessly and pulled off "minor miracles" on our behalf. I invited Michelle to our office after the move, at which time Alan presented her with a thank you plaque and other items to show our appreciation. Another lesson here is to take excellent care of your vendors, particularly paying their invoices on time, as you never know you if will have to ask them for the impossible. It was weeks after Fremont was completed that we agreed on a price with the contractor and paid him for the project.*

Netopia was known as a high-tech communications manufacturing company. The Board of Directors and executive management placed emphasis on engineering and marketing resources. This meant the rest of us were considered overhead and had to wear many hats. Because of my infrastructure responsibilities I worked closely with Facilities and remote office management. I found myself on the on-call list to deal with emergencies and other unanticipated events.

One such office was our warehouse and distribution center in San Leandro. There was quite a population of feral cats near our building. The site manager befriended some of them and took it upon herself to try and reduce the overall cat population. On occasion, she would trap some of them and take them to an animal shelter for spaying and neutering.

One early morning, I was awakened by the ringing of our home phone. The caller was the dispatcher of our alarm company indicating the burglar alarm was activated in San Leandro. They were unable to contact the site manager or any other manager, so they called me. I was told the police had been dispatched and a manager was needed onsite. I quickly got dressed and drove to the facility. Upon arriving, I heard the alarm sounding and approached the police officers. They told me they checked the building and could not find any forced entry or broken glass. However, they discovered the culprit. They pointed to the glass front door and there was one of Lorna's cats staring back at us. We all had a good laugh, told the alarm company to silence the alarm, and then I went home. The cat burglar jokes would wait until office hours.

17

Outsourcing Good And Bad

Companies make huge investments in IT personnel, hardware, and software. Every year, IT budgets seem to grow uncontrollably. Setting aside monies allocated to new projects and employee salaries, the bulk of the IT budget goes to maintaining the existing infrastructure. Aging computers and network equipment need to be replaced, software maintenance agreements renewed, circuits upgraded, and wiring and computer room components need to be refreshed.

Data centers and computer rooms are definitely the biggest drains on budgets. Air conditioning units run into tens of thousands of dollars and since they are mechanical in nature, operating 24 hours a day, and they are prone to failures. Generators and uninterruptible power systems that utilize large storage batteries must be constantly tested and maintained.

What if companies can eliminate their datacenters or not build them in the first place? Enter the practice of outsourcing. This is where companies pay third parties to provide datacenter and network services so they don't have to. The theory here is that since third parties have multiple clients, they can take advantage of economies of scale to provide services at a lower cost.

There are multiple levels of outsourcing ranging from simply renting space in someone's data center to having a third party provide everything including personnel. Sounds good, doesn't it? It does until you take into consideration four main issues associated with outsourcing. The first is reliability. Outsourcers say they can provide uninterrupted service, but this is not true. After all, they use the same datacenter hardware companies use and things can and do break. It is impossible to protect against outages caused by earthquakes, hurricanes, and other disasters. The second is security. Outsourcers have to make sure the service they provide to one company is kept separate from all their other customers. Third are hidden costs. You want the outsourcer to replace a bad disk drive or move a server from one rack to another? Well, it is going to cost you! Finally, is the loss of agility or speed to get things done. When you have your own datacenter, your staff can install a new piece of equipment in minutes or hours. In an outsourcing arrangement, it can take days, weeks, or even months. Companies considering outsourcing have to proceed carefully, otherwise they wind up simply trading their problems.

The good news is that outsourcing has come a long way in recent years. Huge companies such as Google Amazon, IBM, AT&T, and many others have repackaged their service into what is now called "cloud computing." It's cheaper, easy to obtain, more reliable, and agile.

What follows is a real-life experience with outsourcing that one can argue contributed to a major company imploding.

It was early 2017 when Netopia's CFO asked me to provide information on our IT infrastructure, key assets, and other items. I was to do the work personally and not get my staff involved. This was quite unusual, and I surmised something big was going to happen. I did not have a long time to wait. Netopia was being acquired by Motorola. We were going to be part of their division that manufactured communications products for homes and small businesses. It sounded like a "marriage made in heaven." Once the deal was finalized, work began immediately to convert Netopia's systems to Motorola's. First on tap was email and Active Directory.

I recall my new Motorola manager called me to introduce herself and tell me she would be flying out to meet us the following week. We anxiously awaited her arrival as we were full of questions, particularly what Motorola had in store for us. I ushered my staff into a conference room and Kathy introduced herself. While we expected a "welcome aboard" speech, that is not what Kathy had in mind. Instead, she told us Motorola follows an IT outsource model and that a company named CSC (Computer Sciences Corporation) took care of their IT needs.

She then said CSC would be taking over and that we should all expect to get layoff notices shortly. We were absolutely stunned! Kathy met with me privately and said she expected me to remain until the CSC transition was complete. I could either "play ball" or be laid off immediately. So much for my first meeting with my new Motorola manager.

It did not take long for the staff to respond. I received several resignations within a week and it became very difficult to keep the remaining staff together. I transferred what staff I could to other Netopia departments to protect them from being laid off. I quickly learned Netopia's CEO was unaware what Motorola had in store for us and pretty much said there was nothing he could do. He too expected a change in his status. I started my own job search and found there was not much call for 50+ year old IT directors. I was rapidly becoming despondent. A short while later, while I was waiting for "the axe to fall," my phone rang. It was Sonia, a VP from Motorola calling to introduce herself and to say I was being transferred to her department, End User Computing. She didn't know much about me other than I was a "good guy" and was told to keep me. She did not have a specific position in mind for me but said she would work it out and asked if I would remain. I learned later, Netopia's CEO reached out to Motorola management and strongly suggested they keep me on. After all, I was well respected, knew what I was doing, worked hard, had accomplished much, and provided excellent support. I will forever remain indebted to Alan for taking care of me. My wife told me it was all because of the Blackberry I gave him.

Here we go again! By this time, it had been five years since we moved to Emeryville. Motorola made the decision not to renew the lease, so another move was in our future. A site in Alameda had been selected for us which coincidentally was only a couple of blocks away from the old Netopia office! I was told not to worry since CSC and Motorola's real estate management (REM) partner would handle everything. Yeah, right! If there was anything I had learned while part of Motorola, it was they were very bureaucratic and did not know how to manage their outsource partners. They just figured they would handle everything for them. Out of sight, out of mind.

The first order of business was to develop a floor plan. I worked heavily with the REM and my fellow managers to come up with the plan. The managers worked on the cubicle and office layouts while I worked on the computer room, wiring closets, and lab layouts. That was the easy part. Next, I wrote a detailed specification, about twenty pages in length, for the type and amount of wiring, how I wanted it done, types of computer room racks, air conditioning, uninterruptible power systems, equipment layouts, security, and a ton of other details. This was turned over to the REM, who translated it all into detailed blueprints and hired a contractor. There was no way I would trust this work to the REM or Motorola or CSC after seeing the results of their work at other sites, so without asking, I assumed ownership of the whole job. I fought and won many battles with them over how much wiring, the type of wiring, how much air conditioning, the color of patch cords, the number of Wi-Fi access points, sizes of Ethernet switches, layout of patch panels, lighting, etc. I practically lived at the site every day and put in many long hours.

In retrospect, I did too much and should have acted more like a project manager rather than a perfectionist, worrying about every detail. I really didn't have much choice, however, as Motorola had laid off all my infrastructure folks and never replaced them with CSC.

I didn't realize I was bordering on exhaustion. I remember forcing myself to take a Friday afternoon off to take my boys Christmas shopping for their mom's gifts. After visiting a few stores, the boys had not picked out anything—they were having too much fun being boys. Well, that did it. I lost my temper and took them home. I suffered an emotional meltdown. After much consoling by my wife, who knew what was happening, I realized I "was at the end of my rope." She put me to bed, and I must have slept about 36 hours. I started paying more attention to myself rather than the project.

I'll spare you thousands of details about finishing the construction and move logistics. The move went on as planned, and server downtime was minimal. Everything worked like clockwork. On move day, there were zero problems! Alan, the former Netopia CEO, sent an email to Motorola senior management saying it was the smoothest and only trouble-free move that he ever experienced in his career. Motorola's CIO called me to congratulate me on a job well done. I still have several emails colleagues sent me thanking me for making their move successful.

As time went by, I took great pleasure conducting tours of the computer room, labs, and wiring rooms—after all, they were immaculate. Even our landlord's team contacted me from time to time to get detailed information on the building's infrastructure and advise other tenants.

After the Alameda move, I became the Motorola lead for all western locations. There were sites in Washington, Oregon, California, Mexico, Colorado, Kansas, Brazil, and Argentina. (Ultimately this extended to China, India, France, and St. Petersburg, but that is another story.) My time was spent on shoring up the technical infrastructures at many locations since they were in deplorable condition. Companies that Motorola recently acquired were particularly bad since they stopped spending money on infrastructure to make their books look good to prospective new owners.

I recall being contacted by Corporate Real Estate (CRE) indicating they wanted to consolidate several small Silicon Valley sites into a location in Santa Clara. Here we go again! I visited all the sites involved to get a sense of the magnitude of the project and quickly realized the Santa Clara site was too small. CRE thought this might happen, so they were investigating getting the building next door to our Santa Clara office. They were both owned by the same landlord.

As many times before, I got to work developing the floor plan with CRE, focusing on the technical infrastructure. They wanted the new building to be a showplace and wanted multiple monitors in the lobby to display marketing info, video conferencing in the main conference room, satellite dishes, etc. It was extremely exciting.

One challenge was how to connect the two buildings together. By doing so, we could avoid installing expensive network connections in the new building—we would simply use the existing ones in the other building. CRE was concerned about the cost to bury cables between the two buildings, and running wires overhead was not allowed by the landlord. I got the keys to the telecommunications (telco) rooms in each building and discovered 4-inch conduits that appeared to go between the buildings. I also noticed several notes written by telco installers on the plywood backboards hinting at inter building connections. I arranged for our wiring contractor to put probes in the conduits to see if they were usable. Turns out they were except for a 4-foot section next to the new building. Obviously, it would be cheaper to trench 4 feet than across a 200-foot parking lot. CRE was very pleased.

I got into a routine of visiting the site once or twice a week. This turned out to be the hardest part of the project as commuting between Alameda and Santa Clara, right in the middle of Silicon Valley. It was not for the faint of heart. Even though it was only forty miles, it took at least 90 minutes in bumper-to-bumper traffic to get there and 2 hours to get home—talking about stressful! I came up with the idea of driving down in the evening after commute hour and spending the night in a hotel in order to get a fresh start in the morning. The people in charge of the expense report clerks balked at me staying at a hotel only 40 miles from home but ultimately agreed.

One Sunday evening, I drove down to a hotel near the building site and went to check in. The front desk clerk started at me a while and then said, "Pardon me, sir, but you are smiling." That caught me by surprise and I said something like, "Why shouldn't I be?"

She said most people checking in at 10 pm were in foul moods after long trips and just wanted to get to their rooms. I explained I was avoiding a nasty commute which therefore made me very happy. She "got a kick" out of this and wound up giving me an upgrade to a suite.

As they say, the devil is in the details. This is particularly true in high tech construction jobs. One day I was going over the wiring blueprints and caught a major error. The fiber optic cables running between the two buildings were incorrect—that is, they went to the wrong locations. Somehow the termination points in the

112

blueprints were reversed. I brought that to the attention of the wiring contractor. That explained why one cable they recently installed was too short and the other too long. They had already cut the "long" cable and therefore had to order a new one—an awfully expensive mistake.

It was during this project I ran into issues working with a couple of the lead engineers from the sites that were moving into the new building. I discovered the engineers looked down on us IT folks as if they knew our jobs better than we did. When I politely pointed out issues with their lab wiring designs, they were quick to dismiss my comments. Knowing I couldn't win battles with engineering in an engineering-oriented company, I backed off and let them do their own thing. Turns out this was a big mistake. On moving day, the lab managers couldn't get their equipment to work! A lot of rewiring had to be done in order to get their two labs operational. I would never make that mistake again.

After the move was completed, CRE thanked me for my efforts and presented me with a nice bonus check. It is wonderful to be appreciated.

> *IMPORTANT LESSON: It is far cheaper to catch problems when they occur instead of afterwards, especially when dealing with construction projects. IT must be involved in periodic, if not daily inspections to make sure the project is being done correctly. After all, IT will inherit any problems after it's done.*

18

Apply What You Have Learned

It didn't take long after Google acquired Motorola for CRE to reach out to me once again. Yes, there was going to be another site consolidation, this time in Sunnyvale. I was puzzled when I first heard about this project as I only knew of one site in Sunnyvale. That was because we were going to build a 10-story building from the ground up. Google made it clear they wanted it to be a high-performance facility. After all, it would be full of engineers and their labs. Money was no object.

I was asked to focus on the design of the datacenter and the building's network wiring. Needless to say, this was a huge effort. I was paired up with a network engineer, Rob, that I had worked with before on other projects. Rob got to work on the network side, and I focused on the datacenter. This time, I decided to take advantage of a new technique for cooling data centers that I had just learned about. This entailed interspersing cooling units amongst the server racks, creating hot and cold rows rather than having huge multi-ton units that were typically installed on the perimeter of the room. After the room was completed and put into production, the cooling worked perfectly. I never learned if my approach was cheaper or more expensive than the typical design, but it definitely worked better. One primary benefit was that it afforded protection against centralized air conditioner failures. Another benefit was that we did not need a very expensive raised floor.

While I was focusing on the data centers, Rob came up with the idea of using Motorola's own products to wire the building. His design discarded the idea of using copper wiring and instead went with fiberoptic cabling to the cubicle. Engineers had unsatiable appetites for bandwidth, which fiber can provide, so our goal was to have a copper-free infrastructure. Motorola's Passive Optical LAN technology at that time was cheaper than copper, the cables were much lighter and smaller, and used very little electricity. This meant we did not have to put air conditioning or power-hungry Ethernet switches in the building's wiring closets, which was a significant cost savings. While this sounds a lot like a Motorola commercial, to a building infrastructure designer, the POL technology was a significant technological leap forward.

The new building worked out very well. The occupants enjoyed having unlimited bandwidth and plenty of room for servers in the computer room. There was, however, one major problem—cell phones would not work in the building. The steel construction became an obstacle for cell phone signals. To solve the problem, we had to put special cables in every floor's ceiling that acted like cell phone antennas and communicated with our cell phone carriers.

IMPORTANT LESSON: Despite how many years you may have on the job, it is imperative you keep learning. Computers and networks change at a rapid pace. While I don't advocate chasing technology, IT professionals must keep abreast of the new technologies and techniques in order to apply what they have learned to current business conditions.

19

Achieving Success

The purchase of the Motorola Home Division by ARRIS started out like all the other acquisitions. We IT folks spent our time integrating the companies. In this case, ARRIS made it clear they wanted no part of Computer Sciences Corporation and no part of Motorola's systems. Months of effort ensued, and I spent a lot of time on airplanes visiting ARRIS's headquarters in Georgia. It was depressing work, making plans to discard our systems and adopt ARRIS's, but as they say, it is better to be the acquirer rather than the acquiree.

While all this was happening, ARRIS decided to trim its ranks. They started laying off most of the Motorola folks. Why? It turned out Motorola paid significantly better than ARRIS which caused a lot of contention amongst employees. We thought the ideal solution was to bring legacy ARRIS people up to Motorola pay standards, but ARRIS management would have none of that. They would just get rid of the highly paid Motorolans! So, the axe began to fall. I was told to lay off most of my employees. One day, my boss called and said he too was affected and would be leaving soon. He gave me a heads up that I too was on the list, but not for a while since they still needed me. It did not take long to know what they had in store.

ARRIS had continued to acquire other companies, particularly one in San Jose. The decision was made to move the employees and their labs to the Santa Clara campus. Only one problem—there wasn't enough room. So here we go again. I was asked to expand the computer room and wiring closets to accommodate more equipment and people. Floor layouts had to be reworked to accommodate more cubicles and offices. I started attending many planning meetings where we began ironing out the details.

It was in the middle of this effort that I received a call from HR. They told me I was being laid off and gave me a specific date. To my dismay, the date was one month shy of my 15th anniversary with the company. Why was this significant? Once you reached 15 years, the terms of the layoff agreement became much better. Instead of three months' severance, employees would get one year's worth of salary. To be short one month was very painful, but there was little I could do about it.

I continued attending the Santa Clara expansion planning meetings. At one of these meetings, I ran into the vice president of Corporate Real Estate. I had spoken with him several times, but this was the first time we met face-to-face. During meeting breaks, we found ourselves talking about past projects. He mentioned he recently toured this new 10 story building in Sunnyvale and was tremendously impressed with its data center and innovative fiberoptic cabling. He said something like the designer must have been a sharp guy. I smiled and said, sir, that was me! He shook my hand and congratulated me on the great work. He then said he was glad I was on this project as it was particularly challenging. I told him this was going to be my last meeting as the company laid me off. I shared with him my thirty-day problem. He seemed stunned and left the room.

The following morning, I got a call from HR indicating I was being given a sixty-day work extension in order to complete the project. Thank you, mister vice president!

So, the end of my job, and my career was in sight. There was not going to be much fanfare as most of my colleagues had already been laid off and the ARRIS folks back east didn't care much for us former Motorolans. There was only a handful of folks left in the Alameda office.

I spent my last two weeks creating a turnover document for whoever would take over my responsibilities. I was determined to leave matters as neat and tidy as possible. My work ethic would not allow me to simply drop everything and walk out the door. On my last day, I emailed the document to a number of coworkers and sent out the customary goodbye email. Several of my colleagues treated me to a final lunch after which I walked slowly to my truck and made the final commute home.

In the blink of an eye, forty-five years of work had come to an end, and I began reflecting where all the time went. It had truly been a great time to be in IT. After all, there have not been many professions that have undergone such tremendous change, and I was fortunate to be a part of it. From punched cards and huge mainframe computers to the PC revolution, local area networks, satellite communications, the DotCom era, and of course, the biggest innovation of all, the birth of the Internet. I went through multiple company sales and acquisitions and layoffs. I am proud to say that over 45 years, I never collected a single day of unemployment.

I want to thank my colleagues and particularly my wife Suzanne for making this adventure possible. It was a great ride, none of which I would trade for anything. Well, almost anything. Anyone interested in a DHL leather jacket?

Appendix

Recapping The Strategies

What follows is the list of strategies that have been discussed in this book. While there is no guarantee you will achieve the level of success you want, practicing these will go a long way to guide you along the path to success.

Have Passion: Find which technology or aspect of the profession has the most appeal for you. There will be times that the job will require everything you have, so if you are not prepared to be committed to it, this may not be the job for you. Passion is waking up every morning happy about what you have accomplished and enthusiastically looking forward to the day ahead.

Communicate: Whether it is email, text messages, presentations, status reports, online meetings, or just plain conversation, this is the most important soft skill you will need to master. Always remember how you communicate is the primary way others will

123

assess the value you bring to the organization. A poor communicator will not get many rewards or recognition.

Protect Data: Every company relies on their IT staff to safeguard the data and information put in their custody. The loss or theft of data can be catastrophic. Every member of the IT organization shares the responsibility to make sure nothing happens to vital information. A comprehensive data backup solution, a disaster recovery, and a business resumption plan are essential to the wellbeing of the enterprise.

Be A Problem Solver: A primary differentiator between IT professionals is how well they apply their skills to solve business or technical problems. It can be said using technology to solve business problems is the primary reason that IT departments exist. Don't get too comfortable in your job as complacency stifles creativity.

Test, Test, Test: Change is constant in an IT department. Every day, new hardware, software, or procedures are installed. It is imperative you thoroughly test your changes to make sure there is no disruption to the business. Even the smallest thing that seems insignificant can wreak havoc on an enterprise if it is not done correctly. Poor testing is a sure way to earn the wrong kind of recognition, thereby limiting success in your career.

Focus on the End User: Never forget, this must be your primary focus. It is easy to get enamored with new technology, but if you don't realize what value it can bring to the end user, and you don't help them use it, you're wasting everyone's time and money.

124

Many people are intimidated by technology, so a big part of your job is to make them comfortable and productive.

Keep Learning: IT is a profession that is undergoing constant change. New hardware and software appear in the marketplace every day. You must keep up on the latest and greatest to keep your skills sharp and relevant to current business conditions. Don't be afraid of working on an IT help desk. It is a fantastic way to learn and gain visibility to the company. Getting technical certifications can lead to new opportunities but can be overrated.

Practice Integrity: Successful people are known for their integrity. They take responsibility for their actions, are honest, lead by example, practice diplomacy, help others do their jobs, and are open to the opinions and ideas of others. When they don't get their way, they consider it a learning experience and continue to focus on their goals.

Deliver: The guaranteed way to limit your success in IT is to not deliver or meet the expectations of the job. IT people are expensive, and management expects them to "prove their worth" on an ongoing basis.

Manage Vendors: IT departments have a well-deserved reputation for spending lots of money. There will be occasions when a project or outage requires the purchase of something on an expedited or rush basis. If you haven't been making sure your vendors are being paid on time or you are considered hard to do business with, don't expect the vendor to accommodate you when you need them to.

Acknowledgments

There are two people who were instrumental in the completion of this book that deserve my deepest gratitude. The first is my wife Suzanne, who provided advice and suggestions throughout my writing of the book. She also spent long tedious hours proofreading the initial manuscript which significantly improved its quality and clarity.

I would also like to thank my sister-in-law, Nancy Richard Reimers, for reading and critiquing my rough draft. When I initially sent it to her, I expected a simple acknowledgment. Instead, I received a detailed critique and a marked-up version showing all my typos, misspellings, and bad grammar. I am forever in her debt.